RELIGIOUS IMAGERY IN THE THEATER OF TIRSO DE MOLINA

RELIGIOUS IMAGERY IN THE THEATER OF TIRSO DE MOLINA

by

Ann Nickerson Hughes

MERCER

ISBN 0-86554-131-0

All books published by Mercer University Press
are produced on acid-free paper that exceeds
the minimum standards set by the
National Historical Publications and Records Commission.

Library of Congress Cataloging in Publication Data:
Hughes, Ann Nickerson, 1929-
Religious imagery in the theater of Tirso de Molina.
Includes bibliographical references.
1. Molina, Tirso de, 1571?-1648—Religion and ethics.
2. Religion in literature.
I. Title.
PQ6436.H84   1984   862'.3   84-10754
ISBN 0-86554-131-0 (alk. paper)

CONTENTS

No va fundada
mi esperanza en obras mías,
sino en saber que se humana
Dios con el más pecador,
y con su piedad se salva.

El condenado por desconfiado

To Otis, Laurie, and Richard

INTRODUCTION

Gabriel Téllez, the Mercedarian friar better known as Tirso de Molina (1581?-1648), introduced his dramatic works to the public in 1604 or 1605.[1] He continued to produce plays until 1625 when some of his fellow clergymen objected to the profane nature of many of his literary creations. In fact, it was due to their protests that the priest-poet was brought before the 1625 Council of Castile. His defense proved unsatisfactory to the stern fathers of the Church, and he was prohibited from further theatrical endeavor. Officially at least, he refrained from writing dramas, although critics believe that soon afterwards he resumed writing for a period of about ten years.[2] In a literary career that spanned at least twenty years—perhaps thirty-six years—it is estimated that Tirso de Molina produced over four hundred plays, albeit only eighty-six are known today. Of these extant works, many deal directly with religious themes, while others, such as *Las quinas de Portugal*, are of historical nature with religious undercurrents.

The extent to which Tirso's religion permeated his dramatic works is revealed in the proliferation of religious images contained therein. This study will carefully consider the imagery in five types of plays: the *autos sacramentales*, the hagiographic, the biblical, the historic-religious, and the philosophic-religious. Within this framework, the images will

---

[1]Blanca de los Ríos, ed., *Obras completas de Tirso de Molina* (Madrid: Aguilar, 1946) 1:101.

[2]Blanca de los Ríos, (1962) 3:1320.

be presented in three general categories: verbal, allegorical, and scenic. Verbal images are those that occur in greatest abundance, being found in each play. In them can be seen the fusion of Tirso's spiritual and artistic temperaments as he utilized his poetic gift to communicate religious concepts.

Religious allegory is the basis for each of the *autos*; however, evidences of allegory can be discovered in most of the plays discussed, particularly in the hagiographic and philosophic works. In several instances, scenic effects are introduced to aid in the creation of spiritual allegories, producing images that synthesize verbal, allegorical, and scenic elements. These are the priest's most elaborate examples of religious pageantry.

Scenic devices are utilized in each of the plays, although they do not equal the magnitude of the scenic allegories. The variety of visual effects points to the ingenuity with which Tirso integrated his theological teachings into the total drama.

By careful consideration and analysis of the three categories of images, this study attempts to establish that religious intent was not sporadic but rather a general trend within the dramatic works of Tirso de Molina.

ACKNOWLEDGMENTS

To Dr. Henryk Ziomek I extend my most profound gratitude, for his influence was strong. Without his timely advice, leadership, and encouragement, this study could not have been completed. Dr. Ziomek's excellence in scholarly endeavor has been a continuing inspiration. I am indebted as well to his University of Georgia colleagues, Dr. Manuel Ramírez, Dr. W. Patilo Scott, and the late Dr. Alfred Carter, for editorial guidance.

To the state of Georgia and Mercer University, deepest appreciation for grants that cleared the way for research and manuscript preparation. My thanks to Mrs. Angela Pérez Snyder for her expert typing and proofreading skills, and to friends and family for months of patience and understanding.

My husband's total support of the project cannot be overlooked. His encouragement and willingness to read and reread the entire manuscript and share his critical insight were invaluable.

CHAPTER I

THE
AUTO
SACRAMENTAL

In the earliest days of Spanish literature, the word *"auto"* was used to designate works of both profane and religious natures. However, by the Middle Ages a distinction was already being made between secular and religious works, the latter often being referred to as *"moralidades"* or *"misterios."* The term *"autos sacramentales,"* designating one-act allegorical plays that dramatized the sacrament of the Eucharist, emerged in the mid-sixteenth century. They were performed in the street as part of the Corpus Christi celebrations, winning for them the applause of the public, the approval of the Church, and the assurance of survival. Other sacraments, adapted to similar dramatic forms, were classified simply as *autos*. The uniqueness of the *autos* lies in their allegorical tendency, with characters representing abstract ideas or symbols, rather than real beings. From a universal viewpoint, the *autos*, in their allegorical presentation of Catholic dogma, are considered to be the only truly symbolic dramas in all of literature.[1]

---

[1]*Diccionario de la literatura española*, ed. Germán Bleiberg and Julián Marías (Madrid: Revista de Occidente, S. A., 1964) 63-64.

In the seventeenth century, a baroque era, *autos* were in great demand for the annual religious celebrations. Although Tirso de Molina doubtlessly contributed his share, only six manscripts have been preserved. Of these, five are *autos sacramentales*: *El Colmenero divino*, *No le arriendo la ganancia*, *Los hermanos parecidos*, *La Ninfa del Cielo*, and *El laberinto de Creta*. Another, *La Madrina del Cielo*, is of a moralizing nature and is classified as an *auto* or *auto moral*. All are dramatized allegories in which Tirso, the priest-poet, allows his imagination to run free as he presents an endless stream of images of religious inspiration.

EL COLMENERO DIVINO

For a twentieth-century reader, perhaps the best place to begin a study of *El Colmenero divino* (1613)[2] is with the last two lines: "Y la metáfora acabe / aquí de Dios Colmenero" (1.159b). These words reveal that the entire work is one vast metaphor. Tirso's audience hardly needed to be reminded of this. The fact that it was presented at a *Fiesta del Corpus*[3] assured that the audience was prepared to witness an enactment of the Eucharist.

The general framework of the metaphor is an apiary with its hives, bees, and beehive keeper. The Valley is engulfed in sorrow until the Beekeeper arrives to teach the bees how to construct honeycomb hives. The task of another character, named Cuerpo, is to construct the hives, while the other bees are responsible for protecting them from harm. The evil characters, Oso and Mundo, are overcome by jealousy. In an effort to lure the bees and people away from the new Beekeeper, Oso impersonates a beekeeper, promising to give everyone the sweet honey of the earth. Cuerpo is easily persuaded to accept the false honey because of his weak nature. When Abeja discovers Cuerpo's betrayal, she simultaneously discovers that her wings have disappeared. She can no longer protect her hive, nor take an occasional flight heavenward. Too late, the tiny

---

[2]Unless specified otherwise, all dates of composition cited in this study are based on those established by Blanca de los Ríos in her edition, *Obras completas de Tirso de Molina* (Madrid: Aguilar, 1, 1946; 2, 1952; 3, 1962). Because this edition contains all of Tirso's known works, it will be the basic reference text in this study. Quotations will be documented in the text, indicating volume, page, and column for the *autos* and act and scene for the plays.

[3]Blanca de los Ríos, 1:142.

bee recognizes that in her zeal to soar she has neglected Cuerpo. Her negligence confessed, Colmenero forgives her and offers her the lifesaving *miel de Cielo*. As she accepts it, her wings miraculously reappear.

All the elements under consideration are symbols. The Colmenero is Jesus who has descended to earth (the Valley). The *Colmenar* is the body of the Church and the *colmenas* are the branches or divisions. Cuerpo and Abeja represent the two sides of human nature—the physical being and the soul or spiritual being. The body is a hospital for the soul, for without Cuerpo, the soul is dead. Oso is the devil, and Mundo represents the worldliness that counteracts spiritualism. The false *colmenas* proffered by Oso are the hives of love, flesh, and self-interest. The Colmenero's golden hive is a physical representation of the open Church, offering the sacrament of the Eucharist to the true souls.

Within the *auto*, the true meanings of the various symbolic elements are gradually revealed. The most compact essay on the allegory is found about one-third of the way into the work. The newly arrived Oso tells Placer (the Joy of Christ's arrival) that he does not want to eat humans, but burn them as enemies; whereupon, Placer responds with the clarifying lines:

> Ya sé que coméis hormigas,
> porque sois Oso hormiguero.
> Mas no seáis atrevido,
> ni al Colmenar de la Igrega
> toquéis, do el alma es Abeja:
> que un Colmenero ha venido
> del Cielo: mira se escampa.   (1.149b)

This reveals that humans are infinitely small compared to God, that the hive and the bee are symbols of the Church and the soul, respectively, and that the beekeeper is of heavenly origin.

The word "miel" is naturally of great significance in *El Colmenero divino*. The Colmenero is the first person to use it when he tells Placer that he wants to make an apiary where the souls can make honey (1.146a). Placer replies that this seems to be a sweet occupation, and he urges him to begin his task: "háceos miel de puro bueno; / que a fe que os han de comer" (1.146a). When the Colmenero talks with Abeja, he advises her, "saltífera miel de obras fabrica / el alma, con mi sangre, y amor rica" (1.148a). Later when Cuerpo tries to rationalize his fall, he says that even though the celestial "miel" may be "almíbar" to the soul, it is more like "acíbar" to him because of the difficulty he had in obtaining it (1.153a). The clearest explanation of the honey symbol is given by Abeja after she has received the life-saving honey.

> *Solo en esta miel espero,*
> *por ser deleitoso abismo,*
> *miel, que es Pan, que es Dios mismo:*
> *miel sabrosa de romero*
> *miel, que por ser medicina,*
> *y de romero, es Dios.*   (1.158b)

After reading these metaphor-laden lines, there is no doubt that the "miel" is the product and sustenance of the soul. It is the spirit of God, the "Maná mejor" (1.158b) and a lifesaving food that "basta a sanar / la lepra del pecador" (1.155a).

In contrast, the honey offered by the false Colmenero is classified as "miel de la carne" (1.150a), which is sold "a precio del alma" (1.152b). When Cuerpo asks for a spoonful in order to sample its sweetness (1.152b), the implied idea is that it represents the first sweet taste of sin. Mundo openly admits to Abeja that he wants to tempt her with the "miel de vanagloria" (1.153b). When the Colmenero ultimately sees this product, he denounces its false nature: "Llámole yo de alcrebite" (1.158a). Placer attacks it as "trementina" (1.156b) and says that "Toda esa miel empalaga" (1.156b), because it is the eternal fire of the devils (1.158a).

Since salt contrasts with the sweetness of honey, Tirso uses it as an effective image to describe the conditions that existed before the arrival of the Colmenero. The lands were dried to saltpeter from lack of rain. All the inhabitants cried, but salty tears did not satisfy (1.145a). However, the salty tears of repentance have a different effect. When Abeja views the consequences of her lack of vigilance, she cries in remorse. Placer tells her that "esos llantos son sus flores" (1.155a), implying by means of the metaphor that the bees make honey from the flowers just as God refines love from her honest tears of repentance.

The main characters, Colmenero, Abeja, Cuerpo, and Oso, are referred to with various circumlocutions or apt metaphors. A biblical simile likens the beekeeper's life to Jacob's. Jacob's great love for Leah drove him to serve her father, the cruel Laban, for many years.[4] The Colmenero sees himself as another Jacob, serving in a strange land because of his love for the Abejas (1.146a). Another biblical reference (Judges 14:9) recalls how Samson killed a lion, only to discover months later that the bees had made sweet honey inside the beast's mouth.

> Soy león de Judá Real;
> come, imitando a Sansón,
> que en la boca del León
> halló el místico Panal.   (1.158b)

The image is clear: Christ is the receptacle of honey (love), and we are urged to partake of its sweet product.

Other personages in the *auto* characterize the Colmenero. Abeja calls him "Encubierto Zagal" (1.147a), and Placer uses the same pastoral image but embroiders it to encompass his humble, though divine, clothing.

> Aunque es grosera la lana,
> de una Oveja Virgin fue,
> que Dios y Ella la tejieron
> soldemente en Nazaret.   (1.145a)

This citation also introduces the idea of the Immaculate Conception.

The imagery of the "abejas" is stated by the Colmenero as he says, "las Almas, que son Abejas" (1.146a). Calling Abeja "Esposa mía," he urges her:

> que me labres, Alma, la Colmena
> cuyo panal de amor, dulce y sabroso
> a la mesa se sirve de tu Esposo.   (1.147a)

This mystical image represents the union of the soul and God in the formation of a perfect marriage.

To illustrate the ethereal nature of the soul, the "abejas" are created without feet, but with wings, "símbolo, que quien labra para el Cielo / gustos de tierra ha de pasar de vuelo" (1.148a). Without feet, the bees cannot reach earth and its sinful atmosphere. They can only fly over, thus escaping contamination; however, souls are not without fault, for

---

[4]Genesis 29:16-23.

when Abeja relaxes her vigilant attitude, Cuerpo falls, leaving her without a home. Filled with shame, because her negligence had created the situation, the tiny spirit castigates herself with epithets, such as "Avispa enfadosa, Araña, Vívora ponzoñosa" (1.154b).

Cuerpo plays a dual role, for in addition to representing weaknesses of the flesh, he is also the earthly lodging place of the soul. His toilsome work on earth is contrasted with Abeja's seemingly easy flights in the air, and Cuerpo sees no justice in this. In a rather haughty manner, Abeja chastens him: "¿Soy hija del lodo yo, / como tú, grosero bajo?" (1.150b). The conflict is thus established between the body and the soul. A series of metaphors follows, contained in a contrapuntal conversation as the two list the virtues and vices of each. Abeja is "doña entonada," "criada," "hizo de nada," and boring because of her inordinate dedication to the Virgin. Cuerpo also reminds her that without him she cannot function: "¿Qué valéis sin mí, que soy / alma, vuesos pies y manos?" (1.151a). This point is not denied, but Abeja's reply emphasizes the eternal conflict between the spirit and the flesh.

> *Y prisión donde me encierra,*
> *el mismo que ser me ha dado:*
> *siempre hemos de estar en guerra:*
> *acaba, que eres pesado.*   (1.151a)

Alienated from Abeja, Cuerpo is persuaded by Oso to accept the false honey (worldly pleasures). He declares, "Su mosca soy, / hambre tengo; a comer voy" (1.152b). When Oso finally arrives, he brazenly identifies himself in metaphors that leave no doubt as to his danger.

> *Soy el Rey de los soberbios:*
> *soy la bestia que Daniel*
> *vio (porque el temor aumentes)*
> *con tres órdenes de dientes,*
> *en figura de oso cruel.*
> *El que pudo hacerle a Dios*
> *guerra, y competirle el Cielo.*   (1.149b)

He is a warrior, a beast, and king of the proud. As for his office on earth, he says that it is "destruir las Colmenas, / y panales de obras buenas" (1.149b). This idea is paraphrased once more by the Satan figure when he identifies himself to Mundo as "Tigre, León y Oso" (1.150a).

Images are often presented in antithetical pairs, as has been shown in the characterization of Cuerpo and Abeja. Earth is a "Valle" as opposed to the Sierra of Heaven (1.149a), and earth changed from a "Valle de lágrimas" (1.146a) to a "valle de contento" (1.145a) with the arrival of the Colmenero. Earth is war and Heaven is peace (1.145b). The winged Abeja, dressed in colorful clothing (1.146a-159a), is contrasted with the mourning Abeja, bound to earth now that she is devoid of wings (1.154a). This is also an allegorical allusion to a soul with and without the spirit of God.

Like the other *autos* by Tirso, *El Colmenero divino* gives concrete representations to abstract ideas. The spiritual foundation of the Church is described in terms of an apiary: tears of contrition produce love, piety yields a humble spirit, and the two combined produce charity. Abeja expresses it:

> con el agua de tus ojos
> se labra sabrosa miel.
> La cera será de humilidad,
> que derrita el fuego eterno
> de la inmensa caridad.   (1.151b)

The conflict between the body and soul is likened to a poorly matched couple, with the husband keeping the wife imprisoned. Their values are so divergent that they never come to agreement. Placer calls it the case of "la bella mal maridada" (1.154b). The ideas of compromise and the Fall coincide with Cuerpo's character. His willingness to accept the false honey is a compromise, and the purchase of it for the price of his soul constitutes his fall (1.153a).

Repentance, grace, and forgiveness are concretely described through the actions of Abeja and Cuerpo. Abeja repents first as she realizes that because she was deceived by Cuerpo's appetite, she lost the way and stumbled into the *Colmenar del Mundo* (the sinful element of life). Stripped of her wings because she failed to use them (she was earthbound), she has lost contact with Cielo. In anguish she cries for the "agua de Gracia" because "hambriente estoy porque el Mundo / no satisface deseos" (1.154a). Placer comforts her in a metaphorical statement symbolizing God's pardon. The words "saludable" and "botica" suggest that God is the Divine Physician.

> *Si con dolor vos purgáis:*
> *el Divino Colmenar,*
> *que tanto os amó primero,*
> *miel saludable fabrica,*
> *que su Colmena es botica.* (1.155a)

On hearing this, Abeja weeps and these tears of repentance are the flowers of God (1.155a).

Cuerpo soon follows the soul in repentance. As proof of forgiveness, Colmenero offers the true *miel*—"la miel de mi amor" (1.158a). As he accepts the symbol of pardon, Cuerpo notes that "todo me duermo, Placer" (1.155a), evidence of the base appetites' weakening in the presence of strong spiritual commitment. In this state of spiritualism and contrition, the soul is experiencing a new life—a rebirth—in Christ, which Tirso describes:

> *Vístete, Abeja, de bodas;*
> *la pentitencia te dé*
> *nueva vida, nuevas alas,*
> *mi amor te vuelva las galas,*
> *aliméntete la Fe;*
> *deja este ropaje negro,*
> *librea vil de pecado.* (1.159a)

The invitation to accept the divine honey parallels Christ's invitation to His disciples. As He said, "Take, eat; this is my body," the Colmenero says, "que en mi Cuerpo darle quiero, / en la miel del Pan suave" (1.159b).

Though verbal imagery is exceedingly rich in *El Colmenero divino*, exterior imagery is rather limited. The staging calls for one basic set that is used throughout the *auto*. At the beginning of the play three small, closed hives appear with a larger, more elaborate one that is open. Their presence is not explained until the final scenes, but they add dramatic force to the metaphor. In the moments preceding Cuerpo's conversion, the Colmenero opens the three false hives to show that they did not contain honey but death, fire, and straw—symbols of the temptations of the flesh, love, and self-interest, respectively. In contrast, the giant golden hive contains a chalice, on top of which is placed the Host. It is a symbolic representation of the open Church offering the sacrament of the Eucharist to those who seek God.

The costumes of both the antagonist and protagonist mirror their spiritual states. Cuerpo arrives "de villano muy tosco" (1.150b), whereas Abeja enters in gala clothing, wearing wings and a crown of roses, accompanied by musicians and singers (1.146b). After she meets the Colmenero, the two exit holding hands to illustrate the union of the soul with God (1.148b). Later, Abeja will reenter in mourning, minus her wings, to visually reinforce her loss of spiritualism (1.154a). When she receives divine forgiveness, the black garments fall to the ground, and her wings are replaced (1.159a).

The religious nature of *El Colmenero divino* is effectively underlined with music. As noted above, Abeja enters accompanied by joyful musicians. They deliver a liturgical choral chant, reminiscent of those in the Songs of Solomon, praising the newly arrived Colmenero (1.146b-147a). Later, they sing a hymn of praise based on pastoral images, still in a biblical tone.

> *Pastorcico nuevo*
> *de color de Azor,*
> *bueno sois, vida mía,*
> *para Labrador*
> *Pastor de la oveja,*
> *que buscáis perdida,*
> *y ya reducida,*
> *viles pastos deja.*   (1.148b)

The villagers exit, still singing their hymn of praise, while Oso and Mundo, newly arrived on the scene, turn the conversation to worldly considerations. Almost immediately the hymn becomes barely audible (1.149a), underlining the abrupt shift of emphasis from that of the soul to that of the flesh.

The temptations of the world are also expressed musically. Mundo's diabolical minstrels sing a tale of satiated desires, with their lyric message couched in the framework of the beehive.

> *El Mundo, huerto pensil,*
> *a labrar Colmenas llama;*
> *y por el viento sutil,*
> *abejitas de mil en mil,*

saltando, y volando de rama en rama,
pican las flores de la retama,
y las hojas del toronjil.   (1.153a)

The temptation is strong, and the repetition of the refrain (1.153a-b) illustrates Satan's persistence.

NO LE ARRIENDO LA GANANCIA

The general form of the *auto sacramental No le arriendo la ganancia* (1612 or 1613) is traditional. Each character represents one quality that is found in humanity, and all of the character's actions are designed to express the essence of that particular quality. In personified form Escarmiento, Acuerdo, Honor, Poder, Recelo, Quietud, and their associates act out their parts. Acuerdo and Honor are the central figures, and the exterior action revolves around their lives. Each shares the same father, Entendimiento, but their maternal origins were separate. Prudencia produced Acuerdo, while Honor's mother was Fama. While each inherits potential strength and virtue from their father, Honor has to struggle with the weaker traits passed on by his mother. Acuerdo is content to spend his life in the restful countryside, but Honor is driven to seek fame and fortune in the royal court.

On his prodigal journey, Honor is accompanied by his wife, Mudanza, and Recelo, his rustic gracioso-servant. Once settled, Mudanza deserts her husband in favor of the influential King Poder. He, in turn, immediately instigates a conspiracy to kill Honor. When Honor discovers the plot, he recognizes the folly of his life—a life that has no solid foundation. For him suicide is the only solution, but just as he is poised for the fatal leap, Acuerdo and his cousin Quietud appear. They entreat him to attend their wedding feast (the sacrament of the Eucharist). The *auto* closes at the scene of the wedding. Honor sheds tears of repentance and once more finds God's blessings as he partakes of the bread and wine, administered by Sabiduría.

Tirso clearly intended that *No le arriendo la ganancia* be performed at a Corpus Christi celebration, but one should note that in it he also included many quevedesque barbs toward the general atmosphere of the court. All the qualities that a Christian should shun are embodied in the court: hypocrisy, adulation, envy, desire, interest, daring, and power. The wise mentor, Escarmiento, warns that the traitorous Caín founded the first city and court (1.644a). Acuerdo also admonishes his brother that ambition creates devastating discord in the court, as he says,

> Siete cabezas llevaba
> aquel dragón, que pregona
> San Juan que el mundo asolaba,
> cada cual con su corona,
> porque cada cual reinaba.
> Símbolo de los encantos
> llaman doctores y santos
> la corte del ambición:
> mirad vos que confusión
> habrá donde reinan tantos.   (1.644a)

This extended metaphor, which makes reference to Revelation 12:3, declares the court's deadly nature.

In the allegory, the urban, courtly life represents life turned away from God. The founders of the cities are "tiranos y pecadores" (1.644a). Mudanza is eager to visit the main street because "dicen hacen alarde todos los vicios en ella" (1.652a). Poder adds that Soberbia and Ambición are rich merchants of that street (1.652b). In his outspoken manner, Recelo likens the entire city to "Babel violento" (1.655a).

A biblical reference underlies Quietud's plea to leave the court. Seeing the diabolical forces at work there, she comments that the presence of so many pleasures ("tantas vanidades") makes her fear their potentially destructive force: "temo que me derriben" (1.653b). Her words recall the verse, "I have seen all the works that are done under the sun; and, behold all is vanity and vexation of spirit."[5] By example and inference, Tirso proves that "Pastor y fuente en palacio / no vienen bien" (1.656b). The two symbols in this statement indicate Christ and the Christlike (Pastor) and the font of life (God). When Honor chooses the court, he is, in effect, rejecting God and seeking the devil. Acuerdo knows this and forecasts a day of reckoning by way of the antithetical proverb, "pagará llorando, si riyendo come" (1.650a). Just as the glutton eventually suffers from his excessive appetite, so Honor will rue his insatiable appetite for the pleasures and power of the court. In addition, the tears alluded to may be interpreted as Christian tears of repentance.

---

[5]Ecclesiastes 1:14.

By analogy we anticipate Honor's spiritual awakening to the sinfulness of life at court.

In contrast, country life is representative of the godly life. Escarmiento poses a didactic question as he suggests that Honor weigh himself in comparison with Christ. If Christ lived and worked in the country, then should not he also prefer that simple life: "¿ qué necio quería trocar / por los palacios la aldea?" (1.643a). As already noted, the village is called Sosiego to symbolize the soul's contentment once it accepts Christ as Pastor. The inhabitants are divine ministers because "con diez mandamientos / refrenan los desatinos" (1.647a). The reference to Moses' Ten Commandments is obvious.

No le arriendo la ganancia is an allegorical commentary on the characteristics that determine a human's ultimate fate. The choice is left open, but Tirso's conclusion is that true knowledge comes only with spiritual purification. When Recelo speaks of ignorance in the court, praising it as "médico mejor / que de nuestra salud trata," Acuerdo agrees with a reversal of thought: "si es más sabio el que más mata, / la Ignorancia es gran Doctor" (1.655b). Acuerdo intimates that he who is ignorant of God will surely die, while divine knowledge brings life eternal.

Being an *auto sacramental*, this play contains many poetic allusions to the sacrament of the Eucharist. In the opening conversation with the brothers, elderly Escarmiento urges Honor to consider pastoral life, reminding him that Christ was a "labrador." There follows a direct reference to the Crucifixion that gave foundation to the sacrament of the wine and bread (Host).

> *A Dios este nombre dan,*
> *pues hecho segundo Adán,*
> *cuando en su sayal se encierra,*
> *con sangre riega la tierra*
> *y coje angélico pan.*   (1.643b)

The subject is introduced once again in veiled metaphors when the announcement is made of the union of Acuerdo and Quietud. The wedding banquet is "un eterno banquete" which "quiere endiosar nuestras almas" (1.659b). Quietud contrasts this "pan de la boda eterna" with "los manjares que en el mundo / tantos Tántalos engañan" (1.659b-660a). In Greek mythology, Tantalus was Zeus's son whose punishment in the lower world was eternal hunger and thirst. With the paranomastic phrase, "tantos Tántalos," Tirso is able to suggest a world full of humans suffering and thirsting for satisfaction. Because of their arrogance toward God, they are everlastingly doomed to struggle in vain. On the other hand, those who unite their spirits with God are freely supplied with the satisfying bread of His love.

Still leading up to the presentation of the sacrament, Quietud invites the villagers to partake of her feast, adding that Sabiduría, the godmother, orders "que comamos en su casa" (1.660b). Sabiduría is the personification of the wisdom exhibited by those who partake of the Supper in the Church ("casa"). When she affirms to all that "la mesa / de bendición os aguarda" (1.660b), Honor dares to hope for his personal salvation. Other periphrastic allusions to the sacrament are "celestial tríaca," "fruta eterna," and "antídoto del de Adán" (1.661a). The latter phrase also alludes to Original Sin.

Honor's repentance gives rise to a new series of images. Seeing the evil of his courtly associates, he cries, "Estaba / loca yo cuando dejé / por estos riesgos mi patria" (1.658b). This is an allegorical description of a soul that has wandered away from its safe country (God's protection). The "riesgos" represent the enticements of the court, or worldly riches as opposed to spiritual wealth of the country. The word "loco" indicates an awakening or realization that he has chosen the wrong path. It is this realization that leads to the attempted suicide. Acuerdo convinces him that this is not the answer, and that there is still hope. This being so, Honor likens himself to the prodigal son and promises never to transgress "la ley santa" (1.660b).[6] "La ley santa" was and is an accepted designation for the Bible, and by its use, Tirso emphasizes the spiritual side of the *auto*.

When Honor indicates that he wants to return to his former virtuous life, Acuerdo presents him with the rustic clothing of a village laborer in a visual display of his spiritual growth (1.660b). Acuerdo now directs his brother to wash in the fount of penitence before sitting at the table. Honor replies that his tears of contrition bathe his entire body (1.660b). This is a rather obvious religious lesson, restating the necessity of cleansing one's soul by repentance to receive the Holy Sacrament.

---

[6]The story of the prodigal son is recorded in Luke 15:11-32.

Three other images taken from the Bible are worthy of attention. Fearful and somewhat repentant, Honor senses the uncertainty of his foundation. He likens himself to fragile glass and fears that he may break (1.658b), but as he continues reasoning, he convinces himself that he is not as fragile as he thought. It is true that glass is made "de un poco de hierba y soplos" (1.658b), but as he considers the importance of breath ("soplos"), he gains courage. He asks himself, "¿No dio el alma / Dios al Hombre con un soplo?" (1.659a). God's breath is powerful, and the breath of His followers is capable of destroying the ungodly, just as the ornate statue in Nebuchadenezzar's dream was destroyed by a single stone (1.659a). In the biblical narration, the statue represents worldly wealth, and the stone points to God's simple but mighty power over His enemies. Similarly, Honor now sees Poder as a worldly value, which he hopes to destroy with a breath. These two biblical images are based on Genesis 2:7 and Daniel 2:31-35, respectively.

A third image is repeated by the chorus when they warn of the danger of placing one's hopes on humanity instead of on God. They sing:

> Al que de los hombres fía
> sabiendo que es su esperanza
> frágil yedra de Jonás.   (1.661b)

The "yedra de Jonás" refers to the plant that God created at night and destroyed at dawn.[7] The implication is that all things created by humans can fade just as rapidly as the plant did. These images, which are based on Old Testament references, were chosen to lead up to the birth of Christ and the beginning of new hope.

In *Deleitar aprovechando*, Tirso designated *No le arriendo la ganancia* as an *auto*, *diálogo*, or *coloquio sacramental*, correctly indicating a lack of dramatic action and scenery.[8] Scenery is pertinent to the development of the theme on three occasions only. When Honor attempts suicide, he ascends to the top of a rocky peak, where, to amplify this visual manifestation of his desperation, he addresses a moralizing metaphor to the rocks below.

---

[7] Jonah 4:6-7

[8] Blanca de los Ríos, 1:627.

> *¡Despedadme, peñas,*
> *que ésta es paga*
> *de quien pone en el mundo*
> *su esperanza!*   (1.660a)

The peak itself has a paradoxical meaning. It represents the heights to which Honor has been raised by worldly power, but it also represents the instrument of his intended destruction. Concisely stated, power elevates humans to towering heights, but ultimately it destroys them.

When Acuerdo and Quietud appear at their wedding feast, they are crowned with flowers and regaled with song. Again the spiritual union is presented in outward symbols. The wedding song also describes the elements that make a happy marriage in the Church. The chiasmus of the first two lines serves to underline the dependence of these two qualities.

> *El Acuerdo quieto*
> *y la Queitud cuerda*
> *con sus desposorios*
> *al Sosiego alegran,*
> *La Sabiduría,*
> *madrina discreta,*
> *con el regocijo*
> *aguarda en la Igrega.*   (1.659b)

Although there is no indication of the use of an alcove to the rear of the stage, this must have been the location of the Eucharist table, for it is revealed only in the final moments of the *auto* (1.661a). Its appearance is the physical climax of Honor's spiritual regeneration. The sumptuousness of the table and the appearance of Sabiduría as pontifical officer, complete with tiara, join to illustrate the richness of reward for those who serve a heavenly king.

Tirso uses music effectively to underline his message. In court, the musicians sing a *letra* that sums up the situation.

> *Si el Honor por la Mundanza*
> *medra triunfando en la Corte,*
> *no le arriendo la ganancia.*   (1.656b)

When Honor takes exception to this personal assault, the musicians respond that this is a very old song, meaning that through the ages humanity has been led from God by the lure of physical gain. A true spirit never envies this type of elevation, for he knows that true wealth is found only in God. As the *auto* draws to its conclusion, the title refrain, "No le arriendo la ganancia," is thrice repeated by the angelic wedding musicians, or the "músicos eternos" as Sabiduría calls them (1.661a). The music of the angels is liturgical in form and adds to the overall feeling of grandeur in the presence of the Eucharistic feast.

Since the two levels of meaning often cross, there is little difficulty interpreting the allegory. Most of the images are obvious and traditional, many based on biblical fact from the Old Testament, or the "libro de Temor," as Escarmiento paraphrases it (1.642a).

LOS HERMANOS PARECIDOS

In structure, *Los hermanos parecidos* (1615) closely resembles *No le arriendo la ganancia*. Abstract qualities are personified and presented as the forces opposing Christ. To succumb to one of these forces is to allow oneself to fall into Satan's trap. Christ, the embodiment of the virtues of Man, serves as a counterbalance to the negative aspect. Man, made in God's image, is the variable fulcrum who moves toward sin and then toward Christ. At the conclusion, the balance is in favor of Christ as Man accepts the sacrament of the Lord's Supper.

The outer metaphor concerns Atrevimiento, who has been thrown from heaven. With the aid of his friends, Envidia, Deseo, Engaño, Vanidad, and Codicia, he plots to bring about Man's fall. They obviously represent the devil and his angels who were cast out of heaven. Man, in his innocence, is married to Vanity, and as Eve tempted Adam, she tempts him. In fact, Man at times is called Adam (1.1696a, 1693a). Although Vanity is never referred to as Eve, the implication is there. She is metaphorically described in terms that paraphrase Eve's description in Genesis 2:21-23.

> *Oh hueso de mis huesos, carne hermosa*
> *de mi carne, del mundo maravilla,*
> *compañera del Hombre deliciosa,*
> *cuya materia ha sido mi costilla.*   (1.1693a)

After daring to open God's desk to learn the science of good and evil, Man loses the grace of God. To help him forget, Atrevimiento engages him in a card game. The stakes are too high, and when the time comes for Man to pay up, he flees in desperation. On the brink of suicide, Man is suddenly confronted by another man who looks exactly like him. He has come to ransom his life by paying his debt for him. The audience knows that this is Christ, and when the last scene reveals Him offering the feast of the Eucharist, the metaphor is completed.

In this *auto*, physical time is of no significance. On occasions, Tirso seems to be telling the story of the first man and his fall, but this is only a vehicle to present symbolically the fall of Mortal Man. The action moves to Christ's lifetime, while earlier there was a mention of the Christianization of America. Rather than being one unified metaphor, as *El Colmenero divino*, this *auto* is one metaphor interspersed with others, creating a tableau effect.

Scenery is essential to the proper interpretation of the religious images in this *auto*. After Atrevimiento declares his destructive purpose, Man is revealed in the center of a large sphere representing earth. The continents of Africa, Asia, America, and Europe are also visible. An actor speaks for each continent, praising the efforts of Man in promoting Christianity (1.1692a-b). Asia forecasts a future in which his country will be free from the Mohammedan yoke. Africa, too, declares that his country will become Christianized by saying, "la ley de Roma adoraré algún día." With metaphors alluding to Rome as the seat of the Catholic church, Europe claims to be the home of the "trono universal" and the "solio del bautismo." Spearheaded by Rome, she promises to promulgate "la ley del celestial Adán segundo / para remedio del Adán primero." The metaphorical reference to Christ as "segundo Adán" is the first hint of the title, *Los hermanos parecidos*. Made in God's image, Adam was placed on earth. Later, Christ, made in Adam's (Man's) image, will descend to earth to redeem his brother's soul. The idea is chiasmatic, even if the words do not follow this form. America speaks last of the "cruz de amor" that will adorn its brow through the efforts of the Europeans. The image implies the Christianization of the New World.

Images characterizing the central figure are in great abundance. Speaking from the center of the sphere (and this central position is designed to show Man as the most important creature on earth), Man describes earth as being made and decorated by the finger of God. Because of its cylindrical appearance, it could be called "la sortija de su dedo" (1.1692b). He then identifies himself as a vice-God (1.1692b).

In the next scene, Man leaves his throne and descends a ladder to meet Vanidad, Engaño, and Deseo. The throne is covered as Man begins his dealings with them. The inference is that Man loses his position of honor when he lowers himself to deal with base concepts.

Asia lavishly refers to Man as "cifra de cuanto Dios por su contento / puso en aqueste globo concertado" (1.1691b-92a). He is king, viceroy, and governor of the world (1.1691a) and "suma del mundo" (1.1692a). In an extended metaphor, Man is described as having a body of stone, feet of plants, senses of an animal, and the beauty of an angel that enable him to comprehend the grace of God (1.1692a). The angels chant that "el hombre celeste / en él se retrata" (1.1705b). Calling Man a "pecador" and "hermano y mayorgazgo de la posesión eterna" (1.1702a), Christ notes the duality of human nature. He points out that humans are broken vases, awaiting repair by God (1.1700b).

At the conclusion, Tirso depicts Man's complete surrender to God in an unusually dramatic scene. A curtain to the rear of the stage is drawn to reveal a giant chalice. Within it is the Cross sustaining the Crucified Jesus. Crimson ribbons, representing blood, emanate from His five wounds and trail into the chalice. From the cup, the ribbons in turn stream into a smaller chalice that is placed nearby on an altar with the Host. Then Christ speaks and explains that His body is "fruto sacrosanto / deste árbol de vida" (1.1705a). Those who drink of His blood narrow the gap and approach a spiritual union. Christ explains it with an anastrophe: "Yo en ti, tú en Mí viviremos" (1.1705a).

The many events leading up this spectacular presentation of the Eucharist are also expressed in poetic images. Temptation appears in Atrevimiento's taunting "coma y a Dios se iguale" (1.1694a). The Fall follows rapidly and Man loses grace. Atrevimiento claims him for the devil's side since he has lost his heavenly home (1.1694b).

Man realizes the implication of his sinful action, and on various occasions he expresses his anguish in vivid images. He laments, "Hízome mal un bocado" (1.1695a), paraphrasing his own original sin. The word "bocado" recalls the story of Adam and helps create the image of sinful humanity existing through the centuries. On another occasion, he wonders what meaning his life ("juego") can have.

> *¿qué juego ha de ser*
> *si no tiene que perder*
> *quien la gracia perdió ya?*   (1.1695b)

He sees himself eternally shackled spiritually by the "soga infelice" brought by his own sinfulness (1.1701a). He compares his spiritual anguish to the tortures of the rack, with his past sins forming the chains and his thoughts, the rack.

> *El potro del pensamiento*
> *vueltas al alma está dando,*
> *donde sirven de cordeles*
> *mis pretéritos pecados.*   (1.1701b)

In abstract humility, he then calls himself an ass who is stripped of redeeming innocence (1.1701b).

Man's mental tortures are reduced to an imaginary conversation between convict and judge. It is a vivid picture of self-recrimination. At the peak of his frenzy, the mortal sees himself as a thief who dared try to steal from God. His self-imposed sentence calls for a personified memory to be his castigator.

> *mándale que sea azotado*
> *sin cesar por la memoria*
> *del bien que perdió su engaño.*   (1.1701b)

Christ's ultimate sacrifice for human sin is paraphrased when He comes to pay the debts of Man. Man cries, "Los hermanos parecidos / somos" (1.1702a). In symbolic terms, Christ explains that because of His heavenly nature yet earthly form, He will clear all of Man's debts and put the receipt (His body) on the Cross. He says,

> *En doblones de dos caras,*
> *que para esta deuda traigo*
> *en mis dos naturalezas,*
> *cobraré carta de pago*
> *y la fijaré en mi cruz.*   (1.1702b)

Important to the development of this *auto* is the idea that, for those who have fallen from grace, life is a game. Consequently, the sinner looks for a pastime to help him forget. In this specific case, Atrevimiento suggests chess, but Man says he cannot play because he ate a piece of the game (the apple) (1.1696b). Neither can he play ball, for when he tried to gain God's place on the court (Heaven), he was cast out. He tells Atrevimiento, "pelota soy yo del viento" (1.1697a), meaning that without God his life has no direction and he drifts along, being caught first by one vice and then another. In a clever wordplay based on the reversal of letters, Man says that with his dignity gone, he is no longer *Adán* the Christian, but *nada* the sinner (1.1697a).

Man does accept the invitation to play cards with Atrevimiento and his cronies. Tirso must have decided on the card game as a mirror of the gamblers who cast lots for Jesus' clothing. Every action of the players has a deeper level of meaning which would be all but impossible to fathom if one of the players did not subsequently comment on its significance. Envy says they will start the game with a blank scorecard, but Man counters with the antithetical "En blanco no; / porque en negro queda siempre el pecador" (1.1697b), indicating that Man is eternally indebted to God because of his sinful life. The deck, with cards of varying value, is contrasted with the deck of life that leads to the sepulcher where all men, "los Reyes y los Caballos," are equalized (1.1697b).

When the cards are being dealt, Codicia notes that two are stuck together. Man comments that they are like "amigos doblados," to which Envidia retorts, "¿Quién duda que arena tengan / porque presto se despeguen?" (1.1698a). It is obvious that those closely joined symbolize Man and Christ who are the spiritual brothers. The abrasive sand that threatens to separate the two can be viewed as the devil's handiwork, ever ready to cause friction between Man and Christ. The players assembled are all evil forces, and as they draw cards they comment on their import. Man's jack of spades is a symbol of God's ire, and the knight on the horse appears blinded just as the apostle Paul was blinded by the wrath of God (1.1698b).[9] A seven is reminiscent of Mary Magdalene's seven sins (1.1698b). Codicia's inordinate desire to win "un tanto y el resto" is likened to Judas' greed, while "el resto" is explained as "mi consciencia" (1.1698b). They agree to play for thirty coins, and Man comments that "ese número ha de ser / tu muerte" (1.1699a). Again it is

---

[9]Acts 9:7.

easy to see the thirty pieces for which Judas betrayed Jesus (Matthew 27:3).

Appearing more and more like Judas, Codicia brings forth an *Agnus dei* so that he may sell it for additional gambling money. This is a gold coin with the Lamb of God etched on it. As they admire its beauty, Man observes, "Encarnóle una doncella, rigiendo el pincel en ella / el mismo Espíritu Santo" (1.1699a). The Holy Spirit, or God, entrusted the *doncella*, Mary, to sculpt (give birth to) the Lamb of God (Christ).

The price of the coin is set at thirty *reales*. Before handing it over, Codicia kisses it, causing Man to exclaim, "Fiad en besos de Judás" (1.1700a). This is a symbolic act reflecting Judas' kiss of betrayal. Envidia is the buyer, and he plans to take the coin and fashion a piece of jewelry from it. Hearing that he wants to mount it on a cross, Man advises, "Con su luz eclipsará la del sol, si en ella está" (1.1701a). The image transferred is Christ on the Cross, whose glory transcends human comprehension. The game breaks up when Justice of God arrives, and Man flees to escape paying his debt (1.1700b). His flight can be interpreted as Man's soul seeking to avoid confrontation with his sins. Tirso's message is clearly the Church's: repent or lose your soul. This scene is a counterbalance to the one presenting the feast of the Eucharist. Together they give a picture of the two sides of human nature and the two forces that vie for the soul—God and the devil.

In *Los hermanos parecidos*, Tirso constantly blends the scenic and the oral to great advantage. Justice, the harbinger of God, enters carrying a large cross. He seeks payment from Man, the gambler, saying, "Yo haré ponerle en un palo / donde pague puntualmente" (1.1704a). Christ intercedes for His earthly image and takes the cross upon His shoulders. Christ explains His redeeming action with contrasting images of the cup of gall and the symbolic cup of blood. He says,

> Padre, este cáliz amargo
> bebo por él, porque él beba
> la sangre de mi costado.   (1.1704a)

The Son leaves the stage struggling under the weight of the Cross saying, "Muera Yo y viva mi hermano" (1.1704a).

Los hombres parecidos is richly adorned with religious images that are designed to appeal to the eye as well as to the ear. The images are woven around four central incidents recorded in the Bible: the expulsion of the warring angels from Heaven (Revelation 12), the creation of humanity and the fall from grace (Genesis 2-3), the betrayal of Jesus (Matthew 26), and the Crucifixion (Matthew 27).

LA NINFA DEL CIELO (AUTO)

The characters in *La Ninfa del Cielo* (1619) are living images of abstract qualities, placing it stylistically close to *No le arriendo la ganancia* and *Los hermanos parecidos*. The basic idea is the perennial conflict in the human soul between God and the devil. Spiritually, Man's essence is the soul; therefore, the protagonist, Alma, may represent mankind in a universal sense. To indicate the soul's complexity, Tirso extracted the qualities that govern the human spirit and personified them. On the positive side are Understanding, Will, and Memory. The elements necessary for the maintenance of a pure soul are the understanding of God's purpose, the will to turn the soul toward God, and the memory of God's greatest gift, His Son. The diabolical forces that battle to gain possession of the soul are Sin, Malice, and Lust. It is fairly evident that Pecado (Sin) represents Satan, while Deleite and Malicia are his henchmen.

In his famous "Canción I: Cántico espiritual," San Juan de la Cruz described the perfect union of the soul with God in terms of a wedding. The soul is "Esposa" or "Amada," and God is "Esposo" or "Amado." Tirso alluded to this image in earlier *autos*, but in *La Ninfa del Cielo* it is the central image used to present the soul's struggle. Accompanied by her three friends, Alma meets Pecado, Malicia, and Deleite. Pecado charms her and begs her to leave with him. Already, her friends Entendimiento and Voluntad have disappeared. Only feeble Memoria remains. Alma is on the verge of marrying Pecado when Christ arrives. Initially she resents His interference; however, she soon regrets her decision and recoils with horror from her intended groom. Aided by Entendimiento, Voluntad, and Memoria, Christ almost convinces her to return to her true Husband. At this moment Pecado arrives and challenges Him to a duel: the soul is once more tempted to sin. Christ proves to have the strongest shield, and an unrepentant Pecado is defeated. Alma returns to her Esposo, and Christ offers His body as the "divino premio" (2.781b) of her love.

Although the plot of *La Ninfa* is relatively simple, with the message clearly on the surface, the form is complex, with elaborate images embroidering the basic design. The baroque fondness for contrasts emerges, particularly in the descriptive presentations of Pecado and Alma, and country (Heaven) and city (Earth). Each contrast is a variation of the God versus the devil theme.

Terrestrial life is "la humana jornada" (2.763b), and the best way to live it, according to Entendimiento, is to search for the road that leads to "lauro y palmo" (Christ) rather than the one that terminates in "fuego" (Hell) (2.762b). Memoria's observation that life is "una eterna milicia" (2.769b) indicates the eternal presence of evil that stands ready to attack the weak in faith. Entendimiento offers a warning to those who tend to err, saying, "mira que hay vida prestada / y hay gloria y penas eternas" (2.757b). These words are repeated in *El burlador de Sevilla* (1.16). The "vida prestada" refers to the transitoriness of life, while "gloria" and "penas eternas" paraphrase Heaven and Hell.

Christ presents striking portraits of spiritual life on earth when He begs Alma to open her heart to Him. He entreats,

> *Abre, que vengo cansado,*
> *Alma, del largo camino*
> *y de la noche me ofende*
> *el hielo, escarcha y rocío.*   (2.768b)

The "largo camino" is life, but "noche" is that part or time in Man's life when one turns away from God. The frostiness of his soul is likened to "hielo," "escarcha," and "rocío."

Of the two types of life available on Earth (urban or rural), Tirso repeatedly indicates his preference for the pastoral scene. Malicia contrasts the two:

> *Un filósofo decía*
> *que en la soledad hallaba*
> *el bien que le ennoblecía*
> *y cuando entre hombres andaba*
> *solo en los vicios crecía.*   (2.754b)

The solitude of the fields symbolizes peace and nobility of thought, while the crowded cities signify burgeoning vice. Pecado arrives in the country and is overwhelmed by the beauty of the setting. In a glowing tribute to the "ribera amena," "Lirio azul," and "blanca azucena," he admits that it is a heaven on earth (2.255b). This same image of God in nature is repeated by Voluntad as she tries to prevent Alma from leaving (2.761b).

Metaphors concerning Alma range from the simple to the complex. Pecado's first impression on seeing her surrounded by the beauties of nature is of a "nuevo Narciso," a "paloma," and "Ninfa de los campos" (2.755b). Since she seems to scorn the pleasures of the world—a condition he has difficulty comprehending—he calls her, in the catachresis, "Ninfa de los campos . . . / de penitencia vestida" (2.755b), while Christ expresses her pure essence in the phrase "Ninfa de los Valles" (2.765b). When Pecado begins his campaign to turn the pure one from God, he employs the wiles of Deleite. He instructs, "Deleite, tus placeres / le pinta al alma un espejo" (2.756b). The idea of Alma's being a mirror to Lust would be Pecado's ultimate goal.

Inversely Entendimiento extolls a pure soul in this theological-didactic metaphor:

> si en Dios confías
> eres alma racional,
> sustancia a Dios semejante
> indivisible, inmortal.   (2.757b)

Alma also presents an extended image of the soul, describing it as a miniature world where she enjoys the riches of her spiritual kingdom. The thought, as expressed here, shares the lofty position achieved by the poetry itself.

> Rica soy, que Dios me ha dado
> un cuerpo a quien vivifico,
> que es otro mundo abreviado;
> mi patrimonio es muy rico,
> gozo un opulento estado,
> a una patria eterna voy,
> y todo cuanto aquí veis
> me sirve mientras estoy
> en el mundo.   (2.759b)

After Alma's fall from grace when she accepts the attentions of Pecado, she is described by a completely new series of images. When Christ first notices her absence, He calls her "aquesta ovejuela errante" (2.765b). His love for Alma, however, is infinite and He continues to address her as "Amada esposa mía" or "rosa hermosa en Jericó" (2.781b). Later, a wiser Alma excoriates herself: "Ya soy fábula del mundo, / soy escoria de la tierra" (2.773b). Christ, in His unlimited love, will pardon her, and it is He who christens Alma as "Ninfa del Cielo" (2.776b) in celebration of her return to God.

The other side of the coin is revealed where Pecado is concerned. Individual vices are "gavilanes" and "azores" (2.755b). In one passage Voluntad lists those that work for Man's destruction, giving them worldly occupations. Lujuria is a "fingido amigo"; Avaricia, a "mayordomo"; Gula, a "dispensero"; Ambición, a "caballerezco"; Gusto, a "cocinero"; Apetito, a "maestresala"; and Pereza is a "portero" (2.767b). All of these qualities tend to put Man's spirit to sleep and contrast sharply with the presentation of Entendimiento as the "despertador" of the soul (2.757b).

Alma's varying positions toward Pecado give rise to several images. Her first impression is that he is a hunter in the fields. Pecado confirms this when he claims "un cazador soy perdido" (2.759b), but he does not clarify his statement. It is natural to assume that this is the devil in search of pure souls. As Alma begins to fall, she sees the attractions of sin and describes her new lover as "galán y bienhablado" (2.761b). She becomes bolder as her association with sin progresses, and of Pecado she declares, "Es mi amado más hermoso / que el sol" (2.771b). Almost immediately after this, the scales fall from her eyes and she sees her lover in a true light. Following Voluntad's exclamation of "¡Oh, qué espantosa culebra!" (2.771b), Alma attacks Pecado in a stream of metaphors.

> ¡Oh falso amador, oh monstruo
> de las infernales cuevas,
> quimera de mis sentidos
> y de mis ojos quimera!
> Oh alevoso crocodrilo
> con que tus lágrimas tiernas
> lisonjero me engañaste,
> . . . .
> ¡Oh dragón que has derribado
> hasta el centro de la tierra
> mi hermosura, como hiciste
> de tan gran parte de estrellas!   (2.772b)

The simile introduced in the last four lines is based on the expulsion of Satan from Heaven.

Pecado also alludes to his expulsion by way of metaphorical self-identification.

> Yo soy aquél que en el Real Palacio
> del monte celestial del Testamento
> puse mi solio en el sublime espacio
> ....
> Yo soy el que mirando mi belleza
> quise del mismo Dios ser semejante.   (2.759b)

Explaining his ability to be present in so many places, Pecado says, "En siete me divido" (2.760b), a reference to the seven deadly sins. Pecado promises a wealth of worldly pleasures, which exceed the number of atoms in the sun, to those who cast their fate with him (2.760b). The choice of earthly riches to express his essence is appropriate, for it points to the lack of any spiritual value—a fact that the bedazzled Alma is prone to overlook.

The meeting of Pecado and Christ is a confrontation of two powers, each aspiring to claim Alma. In preliminary sparring, Pecado lays claim to immortality and an eternal kingdom equal to that of Christ. He then boasts, "Goliat soy el gigante / de los fuertes filisteos" (2.778b). Although the metaphor indicates that Satan is indeed powerful, the Christian implication is that the simple faith and love of a pure soul will ultimately defeat him, just as David defeated Goliath. Christ in turn disputes the claim in an antithetical image saying, "que eres infame criatura / y yo soy Creador inmenso" (2.779b).

Although Christ and God are often interchangeable in Tirso's interpretation, the following expressions can be limited to God the Father or Holy Spirit. At various times He is "Hacedor y amante del Alma" (2.757b), "Divino Esposo mío" (2.773b), and, as described by Alma in physical terms, a Good Shepherd who feeds His sheep. His hair is "de oro fino," His lips "distillan mirra," His eyes are as doves, and His hands are "tornátiles para el bien, / de hermosos jacintos llenos" (2.774b). In contrast, Memoria sees God as a pure spirit and tells Alma that she can find Him within herself (2.774b). By combining the two images of God—one physical and one spiritual—Tirso emphasizes the two worlds that God encloses.

Christians accept Christ as the Son of God, a replica of God on Earth. Pecado also acknowledges this when he addresses Him as "pastor de todos" (2.779b), although earlier he had spoken disparagingly of Christ as "uno que nació en las pajas" and "este hebreo" (2.779b). To Alma, Christ is "perfecta hermosura" (2.775b). Christ's statement "y yo soy Creador inmenso" (2.779b) is significant in that Tirso indicates the dual character of Christ—as Son and Creator.

Christ's birth requires a new series of images built around the Virgin Mary. Christ tells Alma,

> *Bajé a tomar servil forma*
> *en el vientre cristalina*
> *de aquella paloma hermosa*
> *creada antes de los siglos.*   (2.765b)

The purity of these images matches Mary's purity. "Vientre cristalina" expresses the Immaculate Conception within the gentle Mary, the "paloma." The phrase "creada antes de los siglos" indicates God's preconceived plan for His Son's birth.

Describing the coldness of the world, Christ says, "Nací entre el hielo," adding that He came "al invierno helado, / al fiero y adjusto estío" (2.765b). In veiled terms, Christ refers to the Crucifixion, saying that on the eighth day "vertí / sangre, entre tiernos suspiros" (2.765b). The eighth day alludes to the time that God chose to deliver and recall His Son. The eighth day, then, represents God's next important step after the creation of the world.

As a history of the human soul, *La Ninfa del Cielo* contains descriptive passages of its Fall, repentance, awakening, and pardon. Images dealing with the Fall of Man are most numerous. Voluntad begins the downward trend when he replies, "ya me inclino a vos" (2.760b) to Pecado's flattery. Alma is torn between God and the devil: God threatens and Pecado offers *fiestas*. Continuing the image of a wedding, the soul's capitulation is paraphrased in nuptial terms. Alma offers her hand to Pecado as she says, "y a tu gusto desde hoy, / esposo, estaré dispuesta" (2.764b).

When Alma's union with Pecado is complete, Christ arrives to reclaim her. As He speaks to this "Virgin necia y loca" (2.765b), He employs figures from nature to express her passage from a godly to an ungodly state. The plants mentioned are closely associated with the Bible, for they are named frequently in both the Old and the New Testaments. They evoke memories that range from the early patriarchal fathers to the thorny crown that adorned Christ's brow. In loving concern, Christ says,

> *Ninfa de los Valles*
> *que dejó los terebintos*
> *de Sión, la palma y cedro*
> *por los abrojos y espinos.*   (2.765b)

Memoria describes the Fall in terms of night and day as she tells Alma "en noche has trocado el día" (2.770b). Entendimiento reverts to the wedding imagery as he says, "Y que te acuestas con él" (2.770b), symbolizing the joining of the soul with the devil.

The soul has fallen; the wedding is complete. Christ urges Alma to see the folly of her ways. In an antithetical statement He warns her that the illusions offered by the devil will be destroyed by Christ.

> *verás que los edificos*
> *que ha levantado el Pecado,*
> *se postraron a los pies míos.*   (2.768b)

Alma quickly sees Pecado's evil nature. Asking where she can find her true husband, Memoria replies that He can be found within herself "con lágrimas tiernas" (2.774b). The reference is to tears of contrition that wash away sin. Repenting, she confesses her guilt to Christ, the Perfect Bridegroom, with the allusion "Vuestro tálamo manché" (2.775b) and proceeds to profess her devotion: "El Alma, Señor, se ha vuelto / con su Esposo" (2.777b). Earthly pleasures will be replaced by more glorious, celestial ones. The poetic expression of this reward is couched in antithetical terms.

> *Negra eres, pero hermosa,*
> *te he de hacer Ninfa del Cielo*
> *entre jardines de estrellas.*
> *En lugar del lino y lana*
> *que tu amante te ofreció*
> *Alma, te vestiré yo*
> *de mi gloria soberana.*   (2.776b)

Referring to Christ's crucified body, Alma seeks complete acceptance by God through Christ. She claims Him as her Saviour, telling Him, "por vuestro costado quiero / entrar en vos," to which the Son replies, "como a esposa mi mano / te doy en abrazo tierno" (2.781b). The "abrazo tierno" is the embrace of pardon, while "esposa" continues the matrimonial image.

Upon being awakened to the sinister nature of Pecado, Alma calls on her false friends, such as Ira, Soberia, Gula, and Pereza, but they have fled. Entendimiento explains that when the mind led by the soul perceives the falseness of the seven deadly sins, they are banished (2.771b). Christ is assured of Alma's conversion, and to describe His joy He resorts once more to images from nature: "Ya los rigores pasaron / del frío y helado invierno" (2.781b).

The Crucifixion, followed by a representation of the Blessed Sacrament, is the culmination of most *autos sacramentales*. However, the symbolic ritual is ignored in *La Ninfa del Cielo*, and all attention is directed to the Crucifixion. The Eucharist feast is referred to only indirectly. Voluntad introduces the subtlest of hints in a rather inverse application. She impatiently dismisses Christ and heads for the wedding *fiesta*.

> *Y perdonad, porque estamos*
> *cenando, y siento el rüido*
> *de cantimploras y frascos,*
> *y desde aquí huelo el vino.*   (2.767b)

The phrase "huelo el vino" is the key. For Pecado, the wine goes along with an ordinary wedding celebration; however, his bride is Alma and a sinister element emerges. Pecado is saying that Alma is nearly his—he has almost completely corrupted her. He is so certain of his victory that he almost smells the wine that will be consumed as soon as their union is complete. On a theological level, this is the devil, confident that he has defeated God and already smelling the yet-to-be-spilled blood of His Son.

Christ often refers to His last hours. On His arrival He announces, "con amor vengo a buscarte / que me costaste infinito" (2.765b). The veiled allusion to the Cross is more obvious when He tells Alma, "di en un palo el alma al Padre / y la carne a un mármol liso" (2.765b). By describing the results of the Crucifixion, Tirso transfers the image of the event.

traigo los pies y manos
lastimados y ofendidos
y el costado traigo abierto
porque en él halles alivio.   (2.768b)

To Christ, the Cross is synonymous with Man's salvation or "remedio." He says, "Yo lo quise, porque en ella / salió del hombre el remedio" (2.780b). Since "lo" refers to the ordeal and "ella" to the Cross, the image of Christ dying for Man's salvation is clear.

Each of the references made by Christ employs the past tense or indicates past actions. This is Tirso's method of informing the audience that this is not the human Christ but His spirit as it is revealed to humanity through the centuries.

The visual element is of prime importance in this *auto*. The dialogue and setting are tightly interwoven with the one supporting the other. Except for the initial appearance of the main characters on stage, all scenic devices serve as a reinforcement of previously expressed ideas or images. Those that serve to originate impressions are the appearances of Pecado, Alma, Entendimiento, Memoria, and Christ. Pecado enters first, clad as a gentleman hunter (2.754b). His costume immediately awakens the audience to his predatory nature. Quickly Alma enters, dressed like a high-spirited young woman and accompanied by her companions (2.756b). Entendimiento, as an old man, suggests the wisdom of the sages; Voluntad is in villain's clothes, for she will be the one who urges Alma to join Pecado; and Memoria is the *dama* whose noble nature will not forsake her ideals. The appearance of Christ as "buen Pastor" (2.765b) is traditional and is drawn from the many references in the Bible to Christ as a good shepherd.

The remaining scenic images, which are of a supportive nature, give outward symbols of abstract ideas. Pecado's success in duping Alma is externalized first when Deleite blindfolds Entendimiento and leads him away from the soul (2.563b). Shortly afterwards, Alma falls asleep as she listens to a song (2.563b), illustrating the deadening of the senses as the soul alienates itself from Heaven.

Scenic images also reveal Alma's state of damnation. As she enters in anticipation of her wedding, she is dressed in a black tunic with flames scattered over it. Memoria sarcastically comments on the festive nature of her robe, but Alma seems unaware of her dismal state (2.769b-770b).

With few words, Tirso has been able to show the damnation that awaits a fallen soul and the spiritual numbness that causes one to plunge farther into Satan's trap.

The actual danger that awaits Alma is presented in a grotesque image that proves to be the turning point of the drama. Although Memoria, Voluntad, and Entendimiento express horror that Alma is actually going to marry Pecado, she lavishly praises her lover and turns to seek him. At this point a curtain is pulled at the back of the stage, revealing Pecado dressed like a fierce dragon and reclining on the matrimonial bed (2.771b). When Voluntad exclaims, "¡Oh, qué espantosa culebra!" (2.774b), the image of Satan as the poisonous serpent is complete. Shocked, Alma flees to Christ's shelter. She finds Him flanked by flowers and plants (2.775b) to symbolize the freshness and purity of life that await her. This, too, is visual reinforcement of Memoria's earlier advice: "mira su sagrado rostro / entre lirios y azucenas" (2.774b).

When Alma returns to God, her costume is dramatically altered. The moment that Christ says "Trueca la túnica negra / en alba de perfección," her black cloak falls away revealing a white one decorated with stars (2.776b). This is another physical representation of her blessed state.

There are two occasions when music creates images of Alma's degeneration. To describe the Fall in lovers' terms, a chorus sings of the fickle maid who has chosen a new love and forgotten "cielo." The verse concludes with a modified chiasmus: "nadie la acuerda del cielo, / que del cielo está olvidada" (2.763b). The only other song is brief; Alma chants in a derisive tone to a pleading Saviour: "En el campo dormiréis / que no conmigo" (2.768b). This song is also repeated in ensuing lines, from offstage, casting an impression of the invisible quality of the soul.

La Ninfa del Cielo, along with *El Colmenero divino*, is one of Tirso's most carefully written *autos*. The scenes flow naturally into each other and the images, both aural and visual, play a large part in creating unity in the play. Every image is calculated to serve a specific purpose, and their proliferation succeeds in penetrating the spiritual world.

EL LABERINTO DE CRETA

The historical-allegoric *auto sacramental El laberinto de Creta* was not included in any of Tirso's collections. The earliest manuscript, though not the original, is dated 1638. The *auto* gives no indication of its origin, for it bears little resemblance in style or in structure to any of his other *autos*, being instead an unhappy blending of mythology and Christian tradition. Initially, Tirso must have determined to use the myth of King Minos of Crete and his vengeful Minotaur in the labyrinth to present an allegory of Christ's redemption of humanity from Satan's trap. Theseus, who killed the Minotaur, was to represent God's Son. If this was the original intent, Tirso must have decided that the allegory was too obscure, for a host of Christian references are blended with those of ancient Greece. The reader, therefore, leaps back and forth over the centuries from Crete to Galilee. The Christian element becomes so powerful in the closing scenes that the allegory is completely abandoned, except for the character names.

From the start, Crete is a miniature world where evil flourishes—an "asilo de viciosos" (3.1313a). When it is revealed that Minos has usurped three crowns (3.1302a), the implication is the reverse of God's three holy crowns. Other metaphorical titles ascribed to Crete's leader are "basilisco del infierno" and "infernal Minos" (3.1305b). Already the movement to the devil imagery has begun.

The labyrinth and the Minotaur contained therein are fairly easy to recognize as spiritual symbols. The labyrinth is a symbol of the path of life when it is ordered by Satan. Man wanders without direction, ultimately realizing that he is totally ensnared with no hope of escape: "al paso que más andan / más míseros se enredan" (3.1304a-b). The analogy to the sinful life is clearer when Daedalus warns that once trapped "no hay librarte, / por más que te arrepientas" (3.1304b). Later Theseus denounces the labyrinth in a double catachresis as a "selva de deleites y lascivias, / de errores y blasfemias" (3.1313b), which could equally allude to Hell or the sinful life on earth.

The voracious Minotaur in the center of the labyrinth is likewise depicted in terms that could relate to the devil. Each year seven youths are sacrificed to the monster, who responds with seven deadly sins. The duality of the Minotaur's nature is described in an antithetical image: "lo irracional y humano / casi hombre y casi fiera" (3.1304a). In addition he is excoriated as the seat of myriad heresies against the faith and the Church.

> *Nació en él la blasfemia*
> *de tantas heresiarcas*
> *contra la fe y la Iglesia.*   (3.1304a)

The above lines recall Satan's explusion from Heaven and emphasize his appeal to the bestial side of human nature. The introduction of the word "Iglesia" also shows how early in the *auto* Tirso allowed the original myth to drift toward direct Christian allusions.

Daedalus, the great inventor, created the Minotaur and his labyrinthian home. Minos identifies him as one "en que ofusca el juicio / del lascivo pecador" (3.1302a). "Pecador" is another word more closely associated with Christianity than with the Greek myth. Should any doubt remain as to the evil symbolized by Daedalus, a glance at his metaphorical family tree confirms his diabolical nature.

> *mi padre fue el engaño,*
> *mi madre la cautela,*
> *mi nombre el artificio*
> *que en falsas apariencias*
> *para ofuscar virtudes*
> *blasones sutilezas,*
> *Dédalo me intitulan.*   (3.1302b)

The symbolic nature of many of the characters is not always immediately clear, but as the drama develops, Tirso inserts passages that clarify their roles. In negative metaphors, Ariadne, Minos's daughter, claims that she is "engaño" and a "monstruo de mentiras" (3.1309a). In a revealing soliloquy, she bemoans her sinful, miserable state. Minos had lured the beautiful girl to Crete with promises of joy and freedom, but once there she finds she is his servant. Before her arrival, "Mi nombre era voluntad" (3.1308a), but now that her will is gone she is only a name—Ariadne. A paradoxical quatrain sums up her feelings:

> *Apoderóse de mí,*
> *y soy en mi adversidad*
> *voluntad sin voluntad,*
> *pues vivo sin ella aquí.*   (3.1308b)

The Christian lesson is obvious: He who submits his will to the devil loses all spiritual freedom and spends his life in bondage to evil.

Minos symbolizes the earthly ruler directed by Satan, while his contrasting image is the king of Ethiopia. The latter is openly Christian and

by this metaphor claims spiritual ties with the past: "De Salomón y de
Sabá soy hijo" (3.1305b). Likewise, Ethiopia had kept the law of Moses
until it was made obsolete by the teachings of Jesus ("humana ya la om-
nipotencia del verbo Dios," 3.1305b). The brief scene in which Minos
confronts his counterpart presents contrasting images of worldly kings.
The playwright also takes his opportunity to speak of the spiritual salvation of the African nation by inserting the story of the queen's minister
who was baptized by the apostle Philip.[10] The king's statement that one
Philip baptized another Philip (3.1305b) is a paradoxical image of the
spiritual brotherhood brought about by conversion.

Theseus is introduced by way of the other characters before he appears onstage. Each reference indicates a divinity and is parallel to the
descriptions of Christ. The African king tells Minos that an eternal monarch is coming, "que te arroje a inmortales precipicos" (3.1305b), to
which the evil one rejoins, "Vendrá Teseo a redimirte tarde" (3.1306a).
Risel (a gracioso whose comic form is inappropriate for this dramatic
form) alludes to the Saviour when he informs his friend,

> *Diz que un hombre con su sayo,*
> *con su cáscara y su yema*
> *se mama el diable novillo.*   (3.1306a)

A hint of the Crucifixion is strengthened when Risel asks, "¿será tan
desacatado / que le coma?" (3.1306a).

Minos also alludes to the threat of the Cross when he tells Theseus
that a victory over the Minotaur will not assure his future safety, for "yo
sabré hacerle poner / a la vergüenza en un palo" (3.1311b). This use of
"palo" for the Cross was adopted by Tirso in his other *autos*, although
this practice is not peculiar to him. It is an oft-used image showing the
rudeness of the Cross in contrast to its divine victim.

When Theseus arrives he is accompanied by twelve Argonauts in "la
nave de la Iglesia" (3.1301a). The Argonauts parallel the Apostles, and
the ambiguous "nave" suggests both the ship and the Church, bridging
the gap between the two levels: mythology on the one and Christianity
on the other. The final word, "Iglesia," crosses over to the Catholic level,
weakening the art form, but helping to clarify Tirso's message. The long

---

[10]Acts 8:38

sea voyage had been hard, but Theseus is safely delivered by "gracia" (3.1301a), taken in the sense of the saving grace of God. Exhausted, the voyager rests, and Ariadne (the will) is stirred by Theseus's (Jesus') mystic appearance (3.1309a).

Minos also feels the special quality as he asks, "¿Hombre o dios eres, Teseo?" (3.1310b), but it is Daedalus who transfers the image completely to the Catholic level.

> Porque es nave única y sola
> que de lejos nos trae pan
> que de Angeles se intitula,
> y con dos naturalezas,
> entre cándidas cortezas,
> es Dios, y hombre la medula.   (3.1310b)

Daedalus also reveals another interesting bit of information. As Theseus disembarks, the keel of his ship destroys a serpent, an event that must be looked upon as a foreshadowing of his mission to destroy the Minotaur—or on another level, of Jesus' destroying Satan.

Theseus indulges in a prolific dissertation on his identity, virtually a rewording of Christ's birth and life. Upon arriving, the warrior announces, "Desde el trono regio y sumo / de mi padre descendí" (3.1309b). Next he describes his own birth "entre pajas," announced by the words "gloria a Dios, paz a la tierra" (3.1310b). After a discussion of the gifts brought to him by the three kings, he moves into a consideration of his duality as Man-God. He rationalizes the paradox in the form of a rhetorical question: "sin ser Dios un hombre / ¿como será salvador?" (3.1311a). The description of Theseus's adult years parallels Christ's under Herod. The concluding lines of his speech abruptly swing back to Crete as Theseus declares that his mission is to destroy evil, "tu laberinto destrozo / y postro a tu Minotauro" (3.1311a).

The last speech in the *auto* (which is unusually long and dramatically ineffective) attempts to rationalize Theseus's name and in a wordplay transfer it to a God image.

> Teseo tengo por nombre
> que si en Grecia Dios y theos
> es lo mismo sincopado,
> ser theos lo que Teseo.   (3.1314b)

The weak image is forced and not in Tirso's best tradition.

Several abstract ideas project themselves into *El laberinto de Creta*, and Tirso attempts to give each a physical representation. Theseus's confrontation with the Minotaur shows humanity's spiritual victory over the devil. He shouts from offstage, "¡Alto! a tierra mis soldados" (3.1308a), and Floriseo, in praise of the event, cries, "Hoy el mundo se remedia" (3.1312b). Victory assures salvation—a salvation that begins when Ariadne gives Theseus a thread to lead him out of the labyrinth. She explains the symbolism in a sensitive metaphor: "mi libre albedrío te doy / hilo es que el pecado quiebra" (3.1309b). Thus, a basic Christian formula is again transferred to Crete: Grace plus free acceptance of Christ equals salvation.

Theseus, the Saviour, addresses those he has liberated, using phrases that have a Christian connotation. Not everyone was freed from the labyrinth—only those who had not fallen into the Minotaur's (Satan's) jaws. To these redeemed souls he speaks of baptism, of pure, royal blood that flowed from his side, and of the unifying effect of his sacrifice: "reengendrados quedáis conmigo mismo / unidos al amor que os ha enlazado" (3.1314b). In the glow of victory the redeemer lists the vices exiled from Crete, and these are the same that Christ's blood erased from the human heart (3.1314a).

Within the framework of the allegory, the conquering hero proclaims, "En vez del vil Minotauro, / la mansedumbre os ofrezco" (3.1315a). The religious image is obvious. Following these words, Theseus transports himself again into biblical times, claiming that his deeds, death, and subsequent resurrection are recorded in the Book of John. The forty lines that now remain in the *auto* simply paraphrase the words of Jesus, which are taken from various parts of the New Testament; all are related to the sacrament of the Eucharist. The message found in these words is so direct that it is impossible to consider it a form of allegory. The conscious theologian speaks, fearing that the complex structure may have obscured the original intent. The few images that emerge are based on Christian doctrine and may be considered to be images of images. For example, the Catholic church teaches that the elements of the sacrament, when administered, take on the true form of Christ's body and blood. This belief is paraphrased in Theseus's invitation to the saved persons.

comeréisme cada día
. . . .
el que come se transforma
en el manjar, adquiriendo
casi el ser del que es comido.   (3.1315b)

The final reward of these true souls is eternal life or "tronos agustos / en las sillas de mi reino" (3.1315b).

Of Tirso de Molina's six preserved *autos, El laberinto de Creta* is the sole work for which he wrote extensive production notes. Perhaps this is an indication that in his judgment the allegory was not as clearly developed as he desired. Appended to this *auto* are explanatory notes on mythology and detailed instructions on stage presentations. They designate several scenic devices that aid in the interpretation of the dialogue. Theseus should enter "armado y bizarro" with golden hair (3.1317b) to give the impression of a saviour ready to meet the enemy. The Minotaur's dress should portray him with the body of a man and the head of a bull with two horns that spew fire. When the monster is defeated, a trap door springs open, and he is swallowed up in flames (3.1317b). As the Minotaur plummets into the fiery labyrinth, the Christian should interpret the monster's fall as Satan's descent into Hell.

The last recommendation centers on Theseus's final appearance onstage. A curtain is drawn to reveal the elevated portion at the rear of the stage. There is an elaborate garden and a table covered with a white cloth on which rests a giant chalice. It contains a lamb with a banner and cross. Tirso's direction calls for Theseus to be seated at the table, his armor draped with an elegant robe. The entire scene is one of splendor and richness. Appropriate music further embellishes the scene (3.1317b). Within this setting, Theseus's words on salvation and his passion are easily transferred to the Christian tradition.

In addition to the production notes, a few stage directions included in the body of *El laberinto de Creta* create additional visual-aural images. Minos's entrance in a triumphal chariot (3.1300a) symbolizes the transient glory of an earthly king. Later, Theseus enters struggling with the Minotaur (3.1313b), acting out the struggle of God with the devil. When victory is proclaimed, music is heard from offstage. Floriseo identifies it as he says, "Oye, pues de sus victorias / la música sacra y regia" (3.1314a).

In general, the imagery in *El laberinto de Creta*—scenic as well as verbal—is not Tirso's best. Many images are forced and not in good taste. Others are well turned, but inappropriate for the situation.

CHAPTER II

THE
HAGIOGRAPHIC
PLAYS

Tirso's scholarly investigations as a priest led him to examine a vast array of religious writings. In addition to the Holy Scripture, he studied the various accounts of the lives of saints, especially the *Flos Sanctorum* of Alonso de Villegas and that of Pedro de Rivadeneyra, as well as the many available church and cathedral records. As a priest, he must have shared the spirit of religious zeal that these works exhibited; as a dramatist, he must have recognized that many of the religious heroes were natural subjects for the stage.

Between 1606 and 1628, Tirso wrote twelve *comedias*, each based on the life of a saint—either officially or unofficially recognized by the Church. The twelve are *Los lagos de San Vicente, La Dama del Olívar,* the *Santa Juana* trilogy, *La Peña de Francia, La elección por la virtud, El mayor desengaño, Santo y sastre, Doña Beatriz de Silva, El árbol del mejor fruto,* and *Quien no cae no se levanta.* In addition, Tirso wrote *La Ninfa del Cielo,* dealing with the life of a yet unidentified saint. Since the historical element enters strongly in *La Dama del Olívar, La Peña de Francia, La elección por la virtud, Doña Beatriz de Silva,* and *El árbol del mejor fruto,* Blanca de los Ríos prefers to designate them as historic-religious *comedias* or simply *comedias*.[1] The remaining plays, which are universally accepted as hagiographic dramas, concentrate on the events that surround the saints' lives, while the temporal or political element is almost ignored.[2]

LOS LAGOS DE SAN VICENTE

Being one of Tirso's earliest *comedias*, *Los lagos de San Vicente* (1606-1607?) lacks the artistic perfection of his later works. Religious images are neither as abundant nor as imaginative as those he wrote later; however, genuine spiritual fervor is evidenced throughout this play.

The plot is based on the religious legend of Santa Casilda, an eleventh-century Moorish princess who embraced Christianity. Tirso introduced several subplots of a romantic nature into his play, but the central theme of Casilda's conversion to Christianity dominates the entire drama. Casilda, daughter of the Moorish king of Toledo, learns of the Christian faith from Tello, an exiled Spanish noble. She is quickly converted, after a vision of Saint Vincent informs her that baptism in the Lakes of Saint Vincent will banish the malady that is slowly reducing her to an invalid. Even though Alí Petrán (Casilda's brother) objects, she leaves for Burgos in search of the unknown lakes. In the mountains, two lakes miraculously appear, and Casilda bathes; whereupon, she is simultaneously cured of her illness and infused with the Holy Spirit. As an expression of her devotion, Casilda donates her riches for the construction of a monument honoring Saint Vincent; for herself, she retires to the mountains near the site of the miraculous lakes. In an austere hermitage, she is free to dedicate her remaining years to the contemplation of God's glory.

The plot lends itself to the creation of religious images, but Tirso usually chose to address the subjects of conversion directly without making use of allusions. The most spiritual character in the play, Casilda, refers to religious images the most, although Tello, Alí Petrán, and the gracioso, Pascual, contribute in a small way to the poetic imagery. Most

---

[1]Blanca de los Ríos, 1:315, 1155, 1817; 2:853; 3:311.

[2]*La joya de las montañas, Santa Osoria* has been attributed to Tirso by some [Emilio Cotarelo y Mori, *Catálago razonado del teatro de Tirso de Molina*, vol. 2, Nueva Biblioteca de Autores Españoles, 60 (Madrid: Bailly-Bailliere, 1907): xxiv], but since there is no verification of authorship, it has not been included in the list of Tirso's plays.

of the images in *Los lagos de San Vicente* are formed around paraphrases of God, Jesus, and the Virgin Mary.

In the first act, Casilda delivers a soliloquy in which she considers the intangibility of God and Heaven, as opposed to the physical concepts of deity as espoused by the Mohammedans (1.8). God is "pura esfera de cristal" and "el inmenso mar / donde fin no se conoce." The glory that is an integral part of God is transferred to the souls of all true believers, infusing the recipients with an illumination of spirit. This emotional, spiritual regeneration is expressed metaphorically as "una inmaterial limpieza" and "una clarida que inunda / potencias" (1.8).

On a subsequent occasion, Casilda delivers an elaborate series of oxymorons describing the Divine Spirit. Her images are traditional and have the ring of the Bible in them. She speaks her lines with passion.

> *Dios, . . .*
> *que es principio sin principio,*
> *sustancia sin accidentes,*
> *fin sin fin, todo infinito,*
> *solo una simplicidad,*
> *un ser, un acto sencillo,*
> *una forma sin materia,*
> *una entidad, un distrito*
> *sin límites.*   (2.6)

The Holy Trinity is expressed in several different images. Before Casilda's complete conversion to Christianity, she ponders the implication of three divine persons contained in one Godhead. Her conclusions form an anapnoric paraphrase of the Trinity.

> *¡Tres con una voluntad!*
> *¡Tres con un entendimiento!*
> *¡Tres de un solo pensamiento*
> *y en tres sola deidad!*   (1.8)

Two captive Christians explain the concept of the Trinity in water images. God is like a fountain that springs forth in three jets. The fount originates from pure water; therefore, each jet or stream shares this purity (1.9). The water image is invoked once more when the converted Alí Petrán alludes to the Trinity as "El manantial perenne / del Uno y Tres que ya adoro" (3.5).

In the second act, Casilda continues to be astounded by the concept
of a triple divinity. Even as she explains the idea in basic metaphors, she
questions the paradox of the situation.

> *Espíritu puro el alma,*
> *barro el cuerpo quebradizo,*
> *Dios el supuesto de entrambos*
> . . . .
> *¿Quién vio en actos tan distintos,*
> *tal unidad de diversos?*   (2.6)

The simple human mind was unable to understand God the Spirit;
therefore, Christ was born. The necessity of the birth is explained in poetic oxymorons.

> *Y viendo que era preciso*
> *que un Dios hombre a Dios le diese*
> *por infinito infinito,*
> *humanóse el Verbo eterno,*
> *y redimiéndonos quiso,*
> *ser deudor, siendo acreedor.*   (2.6)

The dual meaning of "infinito" and the complex word order of the first
lines tend to sacrifice the thought for the sake of verbal gymnastics; however, the paradox of the last line is a clear statement of Christ's relationship to humanity.

The purity that is intrinsically God's is shared equally by Christ and
the Holy Mother. Tirso conveyed this idea with an analogy to white
sheep, making reference to Christ as the snowy fleece (wool) and Mary
as the gentle sheep (loom).

> *más puro vellocino*
> *de la más candida oveja,*
> *que vio el sol, que adoró el siglo.*
> *Dando pues, ésta la lana*
> *y él telar.*   (2.6)

This same image is continued as Casilda comments,

> *María dio materiales*
> *y el amor tejió los hilos*
> *quedando entera la pieza*
> *de que cortó el vestido.*   (2.6)

Her words are fraught with symbols. Mary's human body constitutes the "materiales," God is "amor," and the Son is represented by the "hilos." In the paradox of the last two lines, the "vestido" symbolizes Christ's physical body while "pieza" refers to God.

Alí Petrán, astounded by a vision of the Holy Mother, attempts to discover her identity. In a series of oxymorons, he asks,

> Con Vos cándida Señora,
> la nieve que aurora pisa,
> camparada es etiopisa;
> la noche, ella; Vos la aurora.   (3.5)

The sacrament of baptism is of great concern to Casilda. Guided by Saint Vincent, she feels that she has found the path to salvation. She exclaims that on finding the lakes, "sabré que por agua y fuego se alcanza el reino de Dios" (1.10). "Agua" and "fuego" are antithetical metaphors for baptism and spiritual zeal in Casilda's paraphrase of Christian salvation.

The lakes are referred to again in the last act. Reporting to King Fernando about Casilda's miraculous recovery, Tello declares that the waters are "ya medicina / de toda enfermedad, toda accidente" (3.9). On a theological level, this is an accurate description of the healing powers of baptismal water.

On the negative side, Allah is condemned as a pseudo-Christ (3.9), and Lucifer is referred to in several derogatory metaphors. He is "el ¿quién como Dios?" "El ángel nuestro enemigo," and "el ángel dragón" (3.6). The last two phrases are oxymorons, taking their inspiration from Lucifer's expulsion from Heaven.

The two converted Moors, Casilda and her brother Alí, are the only worldly characters described in religious images. The Virgin presents them both in the frame of a spiritual wedding. Casilda is Christ's bride and her brother is Mary's husband. The chiasmatic plan is "ella es esposa de mi Hijo / y tú de su Madre esposo" (3.5). Her praise of Alí as the blazon of baptism continues with contrasting metaphors: "conquistador de ti mismo / de mi imagen capellán" (3.5).

In an image that combines biblical history with contemporary Spanish history, Tello praises Casilda.

Magdalena segunda penitente,
pero cándida virgen que encamina
al cielo afectos que la den corona,
y España la venere por Patrona.   (3.9)

In this same scene, Tello refers to Casilda's conversion when he says, "trueca / . . . púrpuras ya en Casilda los sayales." The words "púrpuras" and "sayales" are closely associated with the ostentation of Mohammedanism and the humility of Christianity, respectively; therefore, the figure is a metonymy that incorporates concrete images to express the abstract philosophies of both religions.

The scenic production of *Los lagos de San Vicente* occasionally demands elaborate staging. Since there is no attempt to achieve unity of place, several sets and complex staging are required. There are seven instances in the play in which scenic devices are used either to introduce or reinforce religious scenes. The first is occasioned by the miraculous appearance of Saint Vincent. At the end of the first act (1.10), the upper portion of the mountain opens, revealing a room decorated in silk, where the nude figure of Saint Vincent is stretched out on a grate over burning coals. His martyrdom is established visually, dispensing with the necessity for any explanatory dialogue.

An apparent miracle takes place at the end of the second act. Casilda's father has been informed of his daughter's gifts to the Christian prisoners. In an effort to verify the report, he makes a surprise visit to her quarters. On her arm, Casilda carries a basket filled with food. The king seizes it, but when he removes the cover he finds it filled with freshly cut flowers (2.11). This transformation of food to flowers must be interpreted as a protective act of God. After this incident, Casilda is wholly committed to the Christian cause.

Production details become more elaborate in the third act when the spiritual element dominates the action. Up to this point Alí Petrán has represented the fervent Mohammedan determined to destroy the Christians. While Alí displays his militant zeal by brandishing his sword among the fig trees, the Virgin appears between the branches of one of the trees (3.5). The effect is dramatically stylized as Alí, sword in hand, faces his religious enemy. Almost immediately the mood changes as the astonished and bedazzled Moor falls to his knees, overcome by Mary's majesty. In this brief moment on stage, the balance shifts from Moor to

Christian as the arrogant Alí is reduced to humility. To demonstrate his sincerity, Alí requests baptism. Instantly, two large clouds slowly lower six angels, bearing some of the equipment necessary for the sacrament of baptism, such as bread, candle, font, water, and basin. At the same time, the tree supporting Mary lowers its holy guest to the ground. The stage is now crowded with religious figures and symbolic elements which converge to give a visual portrayal of Alí's spiritual transportation.

In the last act the metaphysical aspect of the preceding nine scenes is abruptly interrupted when the gracioso, Pascual, claims the audience's attention in an awkward attempt to combine religion and comedy. He is in the mountains with his girlfriend, Mari Pablos, when he suddenly slips and falls. A branch catches his clothes, suspending him in midair. The dispairing Pascual imagines himself to be destroyed by his own hands, in much the same way Judas met his death (3.10). His fears are allayed when the branch slowly bends and gently lowers him to earth. In delight, Mari and the villagers cry, "Milagro extraño," as they interpret this act as a direct response to Pascual's cries to Santa Casilda for help. Containing the metaphysical miracles that surround Casilda and Alí Petrán, this entire episode is a parody on an extremely earthly plane.

Conceived on a more serious level, the last scene is a visual affirmation of Casilda's sainthood. A hermitage rises from the floor of the stage, revealing Santa Casilda kneeling in the doorway. The hut continues to rise until it rests on the highest mountain peak on the stage, giving an indication of the heavenward journey awaiting Casilda. Music of religious inspiration accompanies her ascension, giving the play a majestic conclusion.

Although music is used to enhance the action in scene 10 of act 1, scene 11 of act 2, and scene 5 of act 3, it assumes a more predominant role on one occasion. After Tello reports Casilda's miraculous cure in the newly created lakes of Saint Vincent, the entire village gathers to sing praises to the new saint (3.10). The celebration captures the air of a folk religious festival as four groups of peasants enter, singing in distinct parts and carrying timbrels, flageolets, and drums to create their own accompaniment. The purpose of this scene is to show how the influence of Casilda's saintliness has permeated both royalty and peasantry.

Los lagos de San Vicente is of interest because it indicates the direction (stylistically) that Tirso will follow and perfect in his later religious dramatizations. The profane and religious elements, so awkwardly joined here, will be united with more artistic and dramatic skill in later hagiographic plays.

THE *SANTA JUANA* TRILOGY

Tirso de Molina based the *Santa Juana* trilogy (1613-1614) on the remarkable life of Juana de la Cruz, a Franciscan nun whose saintly existence inspired numerous poets and religious writers. She was born in 1481 in the tiny village of Cubas, near Toledo, and died in 1534. Since her miracles and ecstasies were widely recognized, the Church has given her the title *beata*; however, it has not yet seen fit to canonize her. Tirso undoubtedly read many accounts of Juana's life, including her biography written by Fray Antonio Daza.[3] Cotarelo y Mori found that Tirso's actual source materials were the *Memorias* of Sor María Evangelista, Juana's companion at the convent.[4] It is interesting to note that Tirso introduced María Evangelista as one of the supporting characters in the trilogy.

The general pattern of the trilogy proceeds in a natural rhythm. The initial *comedia* deals with Juana's first encounters with the metaphysical world. The second is an account of her years as abbess of her convent when her mystic powers are fully developed. It is in this part that religious imagery bursts forth in unbridled profusion. The final *comedia* deals with Juana's last years on earth. Worldly elements are in predominance until the final act, when scenes of celestial inspiration lead to her glorious ascension to Heaven. Elaborating on Tirso's image of death as night,[5] one may consider the three parts as morning, noon, and night: the beginning of her life, the full development in her middle years, and her death.

La Santa Juana: Part I

The first *comedia* in the *Santa Juana* trilogy deals with Santa Juana's early life, when her special mystic powers were beginning to be recognized. In the play's opening scene, the thirteen-year-old Juana is god-

---

[3]Blanca de los Ríos, 1:728.

[4]Cotarelo y Mori, 2:xxxvi.

[5]*La Santa Juana: Part III*, act 3, scene 14.

mother at a peasant wedding. A nobleman is smitten by her beauty and asks for her hand. To her father's dismay, Juana refuses and flees to the monastery. San Francisco gives her heavenly assistance, and once she comes within the shelter of the religious house, her father grudgingly relents, fearing that he may offend God. Juana enters the Franciscan order, and within three years her zealous nature and pure spirit earn her the position of abbess. During this time, Juana experiences direct confrontations with her guardian angel, saints of the Church, and even with Christ, who supplies miraculous answers to her prayers. Her ecstasies become frequent as her spiritual bonds grow stronger. The *comedia* closes with Juana's miraculous transportation to Heaven.

Images woven around Juana are in abundance. At the wedding, she is described by a guest as being more divine than human (1.2). Speaking of her open devotion to God and His Church, another guest refers to her as "Espejo de la Sagra de Toledo" (1.16). All accept that the young girl is God's spokeswoman: "el espíritu hable / de Dios por su boca" (3.12).

Reflecting on her own life, Juana employs a wordplay based on her natal village to express her dedication to God: "En Azaña me dio el ser / Dios: hazañas he de hacer" (2.7). At the monastery, Juana assumes the appellation Juana de la Cruz in praise of the House of the Cross that offers protection in God's name.

Juana's close relationship with her spiritual Father (God) and her Husband (Christ) causes her to tell her earthly father that "el alma me ha renovado" and "Ya no soy mía: adiós, padre" (2.21). The sisters in the convent also sense her unique quality calling her "santa" (3.5), "Angel," "Cielo" (2.22), and "serafín" (2.21).

A single discordant note appears when Evangelista, the *Maestra de novicias*, is consumed by jealousy. While others adore Juana's virtues, the *Maestra* can only visualize them as a threat to her own aspiration to the position of abbess. Of her rival she snaps, "Todo aquello es santo y bueno, pero para mí es veneno" (3.2). She expresses her emotions with intense images: "En un infierno estoy de envidia" and "las telas del corazón / alguna sierpe me come" (3.13). In the same scene Evangelista admits that her jealousy is synonymous with the devil: "No es el Espíritu Santo / quien habla sino el Demonio."

Juana, however, sees herself as "la herencia pecadora" (3.2) and determines to increase her scourgings to further purify her soul (3.3). Shortly thereafter, Juana refers to the duality of her nature in terms of

Martha and Mary, the sisters whose lives epitomize the body and soul, respectively.[6] Juana observes,

> *Bien puede hallarse María*
> *entre los brazos de Marta.*
> *El alma contemple y parta*
> *al Cielo, pues con Dios priva,*
> *y el cuerpo, que es Marta activa,*
> *trabaje.*   (3.6)

Images concerning God and Christ (whose identities are interchangeable) are nearly always constructed within the framework of a mystic marriage metaphor. Juana tells her father that God will be her "esposo" and his "buen yerno / sin pobreza, sin mudanza" (2.1). She rejects marriage, saying,

> *no queréis, padre, vos*
> *darme por esposo un hombre*
> *cuando lo quiere ser Dios.*   (2.1)

Actually, God is all the family that Juana needs. Besides being her "Esposo Eterno" (2.7), God is

> Padre: *a Dios por padre tengo;*
> Tío: *Dios solo es mi tío;*
>   *Dios es mi esposo y mi dueño.*   (2.18)

In the opening lines of *La Santa Juana*, a peasant reverently offers, "que el amor es Dios y aspira a lo infinito" (1.1). The closing scene echoes this same idea with the guardian angel's image of God as "Autor eterno de gracia" (3.23). The intervening scenes are permeated with this same idea of ultimate praise. In prayer, Juana confides,

> *Casarme quieren, mi Dios,*
> *siendo cosa reprobada*
> *el ser dos veces casada*
> *y siendo mi Esposo Vos.*   (1.7)

---

[6]Luke 10:38-42.

In effect, she is saying that her spiritual union with God would make any physical union impossible, since it would constitute bigamy. She repeats this philosophy to her father when she tells him that Christ lives in her soul as *Esposo*. He is king; therefore, she is queen (2.21).

For Juana, the religious habit is an outward sign of her spiritual union. The promise that she will soon be adorned with the finery of her eternal wedding is an allusion to the novitiate's robe (2.16). The marriage analogy is further developed as Tirso contrasts the spiritual marriage with the worldly one. Loarte, the proposed husband, is a "lobo" to his prospective bride, and she herself is an "oveja" (2.13). The implication is that marriage will destroy her just as the wolf devoured the lamb. Using the word "cruz," Tirso fashions images that continue the same line of reasoning. The "cruz de matrimonio" is destructive, but the "Cruz de Dios" offers sublime happiness (2.16). This being so, true happiness for Juana can be found only in Christ: "Esposo de inmenso nombre" (3.22).

The founder of the Franciscan monastery, in which the terrified bride-to-be finds shelter, is often mentioned through poetic images. He is "Seráfico peregrino" (2.3), an ambassador of Christ, and master-of-arms in the monastery (2.18). When he appears before Juana along with Santo Domingo, she calls him "Divino Predicador" and the one whom she obeys as she would a father. In a series of metaphors, Juana eulogizes him.

> *Vos sois mi santo, mi padre,*
> *mi refugio, mi remedio,*
> *mi regalo, mi descanso,*
> *y así vuestro sayal queiro.*   (2.23)

The *sayal* or Franciscan robe is most significant in *La Santa Juana: Part I*. It suddenly appears, as if miraculously sent from heaven, when Juana decides to escape from Loarte (2.3). She sees it as God's way of telling her to go to the monastery of that particular order. Once clothed in the simple Franciscan habit, she senses that it has an interlining of jewels and fine brocade (2.18). Alluding to the inner spiritual wealth that the robe has brought her, she says, "éste es brocado; / no es, padre, sayal grosero" (2.15).

The Dominican habit also has a symbolic interpretation, which Santo Domingo explains as he seeks to enlist Juana in his order. The white scapulary symbolizes the virginal purity of God, the black robe indicates mourning for the world, and the rosary points to devotion (2.23). Juana admires the habit's dramatic beauty, but her preference is still the "pobres remiendos" of the Franciscans, which she links with Christ's wounds in this simile:

> *estos pobres remiendos,*
> *que, como las cinco llagas,*
> *aunque pobre guarnecieron*
> *con sus rubíes el sayal*
> *de Francisco, es ya sin precio.*   (2.23)

The loose construction of the play allows for, and even expects, a certain amount of extraneous action. While not directly essential, each event in *La Santa Juana* is chosen to underline spiritual values. A secondary plot deals with jealousy, mistrust, and conspiracy in the marriage between Marco Antonio and the devoted Leonor. The implied message is that a bride joined to the Ideal Husband (God) experiences only joy and exultation, and this union is superior to any other on earth.

Act 1 concludes with a long, allegorical dissertation by Juana about Santa Inés (1.16). As the story of her life unfolds, it is easy to compare her life to Juana's. Like Juana, Inés began her spiritual life at the age of thirteen by encountering the Virgin in a vision and receiving physical proof of her divine visitor. She, too, founded a nunnery and a church and became an abbess at an early age. Inés, however, fell from grace when she succumbed to the temptation of the flesh. Her subsequent repentance restored her to God's favor. Whether Juana will suffer the same temptation is not revealed in Part I. Within this allegory there are several sensitive figures. Inés's prayers are transported to pastoral images as she describes her life as a shepherdess.

> *postrada por la tierra*
> *apacentaba el alma*
> *con el precioso néctar*
> *de la oración sabrosa.*   (1.16)

The Virgin is addressed as "Hermosa hembra," "gloriosa Reina," and "Madre de clemencia." Concerning Jesus and His death, the evil that led to His Crucifixion is paraphrased in the following manner:

caerán del Cielo piedras
envueltas en la sangre
que verterán sus venas.   (1.16)

Tirso used music, specifically song, to heighten the religious atmosphere on two separate occasions. Before leaving her village, Juana attends a religious festival, where singing laborers praise the Virgin and extol the beauty of the land as an example of God's handiwork. A soloist renders this summation: "Hízola el divino Autor / del Cielo la repostera" (1.13). The pattern is similar to a choral chant with *a capella* delivery.

Act 2 contains one abbreviated scene in which celestial voices forecast the arrival of God's bride at the Franciscan monastery. The last stanza is a restatement of the mystic union. Juana is a dove, symbol of love and purity, and God is the husband. They sing,

Paloma escogida:
tu Esposo te llama
para aposentarte
dentro de su alma.   (2.16)

Besides the Franciscan robe, other accessories in *La Santa Juana: Part I* lend themselves to the development of the play. Loarte's pre-wedding gifts ("galas") contribute to an antithetical scene that contrasts Christ's gifts with Loarte's (2.3). The cork-soled sandals are the embodiment of pride and vanity, and the gold chains, despite their beauty, are as iron to her, for their capricious value would chain her heart away from Christ. Rejecting the finery, she seeks refuge from the vain world in the monastery. Figuratively, the world is a sea and her ship is God's house.

El mundo es un mar que combate
con alas de vituperio.
Nave será un monasterio
si el Cielo el paso me allana.   (2.3)

Juana rejects the gifts, and they disappear through a trap door. At the same time a Franciscan habit is thrown onstage, and a voice, ostensibly God's, says, "Estas son mis galas, Juana" (2.3). The word "galas" has now passed from a worldly connotation to the sublime or from "un disfraz a lo divino." She seizes the cord of the robe and declares her devotion to it in this modified chiasmus: "que aunque está roto este saco / no lo echaré en saco roto" (3.3).

During Juana's first months at the monastery, she is charged with guarding the message box at the main door. The devout young girl imagines that the box is a cradle for the holy baby and rocks it as if the child were there. Then, looking, she discovers that He has materialized (3.6). The implication is that true devotion can work miracles. The cradle disappears, and as church bells ring, the monastery wall cracks, revealing a chalice with the baby Jesus, a visual paraphrase of the incident at the door.

Two other props transmit strong images of Juana's special powers. An earthenware vessel is miraculously repaired at Juana's request (3.2), and the rosaries that she presented for Christ's blessing have special powers. Speaking of one of the rosaries, San Laurel makes this hyperbolic statement:

> gana tantos perdones
> como hay hojas, flores, plantas
> media legua alrededor
> y las indulgencias propias
> de Asís, famosa en Italia.   (3.23)

Several incidents within this play merit special consideration, for they are used externalize emotional experiences. On the road to the monastery, Loarte spies his bride-to-be and attempts to embrace her, but Juana disappears (2.13). This can be interpreted as the protection God offers when escape seems impossible. At the monastery, Vásquez attempts to pull his daughter away, but she clings to the sisters (2.18). Her act is that of a soul torn between the earthly and the heavenly. Later in the scene, when Juana is surrounded by the nuns, she feels crowded and longs to communicate with God. She cries out to Him and is suddenly swept away in an outward display of spiritual escape from the world.

The appearance of the guardian angel further visualizes spiritual movement. He first appears in act 1, scene 4, identifying himself as her special communicative agent with Christ. The conversation between the two mirrors their spiritual relationship. Later, his words, "Siempre estoy, Juana, a tu lado" (3.15), allude to the heavenly protection offered to consecrated souls. On another occasion San Laurel requests her intercession on behalf of the souls in Purgatory (3.16). The scene has a dual purpose: it indicates the importance of intercession, as well as the continued celestial favor enjoyed by Santa Juana.

The last scene in *La Santa Juana* is a synthesis of music, scenery, props, and dialogue—all calibrated to endow earth with a heavenly tone. It commences with the entrance of all of the nuns in the monastery, who kneel as celestial music plays. At this moment of reverence a rear alcove is unveiled, revealing Christ seated on a throne. Many angels surround Him, and one is at His feet (Juana's guardian angel) presenting the chest full of rosaries. As soon as Christ blesses the beads, the alcove is covered and the guardian angel descends to Juana (3.23). The action thus far has illustrated the manner in which Christ receives petitions from His angels. The final thirty-seven lines again externalize the relationship between Juana and the guardian angel. As a reward for her efforts on behalf of the souls in Purgatory, he promises to take her to Christ, and she instantly disappears. The intent is to show, physically, a spiritual transportation or mystic union of the soul with God. On this ecstatic note the play concludes.

La Santa Juana: Part II

The second play in the *Santa Juana* trilogy deals with the Franciscan nun's most active period. Several years have lapsed since the close of the first *comedia*, and Juana has enjoyed the position of abbess for some time. The opening scenes dwell briefly on the religious climate of the day, which is especially directed toward the threat of the Lutherans. The main plot, however, develops when Carlos V arrives with his nephew, Jorge of Aragon, a member of the Order of Santiago and the new *comendador* of Cubas—Juana's village. The villagers soon discover that the nephew inherited none of his uncle's nobility. Though married, he ardently pursues a local lass, Mari Pascuala. After one unsuccessful attempt to resist his attention, Mari strengthens her resolve and enters Juana's monastery as a Franciscan novitiate. When Jorge attempts to lure Mari away again, Juana reminds him that his day of reckoning is approaching. He suddenly repents, and on the next day he dies.

A second plot, which is equally important, is closely intertwined with the first. The *vicaria*, who still burns with jealousy, accuses Juana of meddling in affairs outside her domain (specifically, Jorge's activities) and of allowing the monastery to lapse into a state of poverty. The provincial father blindly accepts the assistant superior's testimony and sentences Juana to be stripped of her veil, placed on the rack, whipped, and imprisoned in her cell. Juana accepts this in a spirit of humility, believing such lamentable treatment to be deserved. While her physical life is less than happy, her spiritual being is ecstatic. She has frequent meetings with her guardian angel, three encounters with Jesus, and one with Saint Francis. The two plots converge with the death of the assistant superior and the arrival of Carlos V. The king promises that Cubas will have no other *comendador* save the monarch himself, and in recognition of Juana's extraordinary spirituality, he praises her as the glory of Spain.

The simple framework of the play is free from extraneous events and characters. The moments of humor that are centered around Jorge's gracioso, Lillo, offer necessary relief from the concentrated emotionalism that dominates most of the play. In contrast, the staging and dialogue are exceedingly elaborate, with numerous scenic and aural images.

Tirso introduced a variety of images to characterize the figure of Juana. On the negative side are the vitriolic comments of the assistant superior as she attempts to besmirch her rival's reputation. In a chiaroscuro figure, she attacks the sainted nun as "demonio en forma de ángel de luz" (1.7). The same idea of her hypocritical nature is expressed when her detractor says, "el lobo se finge oveja" (2.5).

On the positive side, Juana is called "monja vieja en la inocencia" (1.9). The underlying belief is that only age brings spiritual purification. Juana, though still young, has achieved this state of innocence. She partially explains her ability to resist worldly contamination in concrete images. Her faith is a protective armor that constantly shields her from evil; however, when temptation approaches she reinforces her armor with a hair shirt. Metaphorically, the thorny fabric of the garment forms a stairway to God's throne. The path ("escalas") to God may not be smooth, but the reward is more than worth the hardship endured on earth. The contrast between Heaven and earth is clearly indicated in the following words:

> *¿No tengo ya una cota hecha de malla?*
> *A vestirme yo. Contra los vicios*
> *corona tiene Dios: para alcanzalla*
> *no son malas escalas los cilicios;*
> *por espinas da Dios sillas divinas.*
> *Al arma Juana, pues, busca espinas.*   (1.15)

Knowing that Juana will undergo persecution at the hands of the *vi-caria*, her guardian angel tells her that it will be a test of her faith: "como a Job, probarte intenta" (1.9). Santa Juana presents a more complex analogy as she braces herself for her trials. First she establishes the point that as Jesus' spiritual wife, she shares all of her husband's joys and pains. If Jesus suffered at the hands of His enemies and yet loved them, she will do likewise. She is confident that God will support her just as He sustained Moses when he suffered among the thorns and brambles. Juana's double analogy to Christ and to Moses is contained in the following lines.

> *que si amó a los enemigos,*
> *porque en ellos halló el bien*
> *de las penas, yo también*
> *sigo sus plantas divinas,*
> *pues entre zarzas y espinas*
> *Dios apareció a Moisén.*   (1.9)

On various occasions, Juana's actions and words emulate her Christian humility. She sees herself as an erring human deserving of any punishment meted out to her. She confesses her unworthiness to the vindictive *vicaria*, concluding her deprecatory remarks by humbly requesting permission to kiss her superior's feet (2.4). As their conversation continues, Juana speaks of her punishment which she considers to be partial payment for the sacrifice of Jesus' life. In comparison to Jesus' crucifixion, her scourgings are insignificant, and she makes this analogy:

> *Es justo*
> *que a Dios pague en la moneda*
> *que pagó por mis pecados;*
> *cinco mil azotes fueran*
> *más justos en mí que en El.*   (2.5)

In addition to being a receptacle for humility, Juana is the embodiment of nearly divine forgiveness. When she learns of the impending death of the abbess (formerly the *vicaria*), Juana intercedes in her behalf as she prays, "Dalda doloroso llanto / y muera con contrición" (3.2). Hearing her Christlike petition, one of the nuns is moved to comment in an antithetical simile, "murió la que os perseguía / como un ángel!" (3.13).

Both Mari Pascuala and Jorge are sinners who repent and regain God's favor. Most of the time Jorge is the devil's representative of lust, while Mari is his victim. Tirso intended to show a direct relationship between Mari and Eve, for when the girl is tempted by her lover, she asks, "si a Eva vence una manzana, / que hoy a mí me venza un hombre" (2.10). Jorge's first confrontation with Mari Pascuala is an allegory of the flesh being tempted by lust (1.11). The image of water is employed in such a manner that it has two, and possibly three, interpretations. For Jorge it symbolizes satisfaction of his lust, causing him to utter the sacrilegious "Agua, Dios" to Mari when he seeks the water that would quench his carnal thirst. The Christian interpretation of his words suggests the purifying baptismal waters, contrasting with the commander's base intentions. Being natively good, Mari Pascuala knows that yielding will bring harm to both of them. She indicates this in veiled words.

> Estará sudando, pues,
> y beber agua sudando,
> matarále.   (1.11)

Later, Jorge's successful kidnapping of the girl is an external representation of a soul being stolen from God (1.21). Mari manages to escape her captor, and for a time she finds refuge in the monastery with Santa Juana. But the latter soon advises, "Fuerza es, hija, que volváis / a casa de vuestro padre" (2.3). Her words can be interpreted on two levels: Mari should return to her earthly father's home, but, more importantly, she must return to her Heavenly Father's house and forsake her sinful habits. To direct her toward God, Juana compares Christ with Jorge, the commander (2.3). Each wears a cross—Christ's is the rugged burden carried on His back, while that of Jorge, bedecked with jewels, adorns his chest. Since the power of Christ's Cross is undisputed, making Him the *Gran Maestre*, would not Mari be wiser to prefer His love over that of the inferior commander? Mari agrees, but the flesh proves to be weaker than the spirit, causing her to yield once more. Her return to the convent, however, is almost immediate, and she takes the first religious vows to demonstrate her sincerity. Jorge, described as a wolf in sheep's clothing (3.14), determines to entice his prey once more. He sends her a love letter, hidden in a basket of apples. Seeing the fruit, a symbol of temptation that dates back to Adam and Eve, Mari exclaims, "es Don Jorge la serpiente / que engaña con fruta a Eva!" (3.6).

Jorge's repentance is triggered by ambiguous, allegorical conversation with his servant (3.8). While Lillo is asleep, he babbles about a dice game, but Jorge thinks he is talking about a wager concerning his own eternal punishment. The commander is shaken but recovers; however, his composure is destroyed almost immediately when Juana appears, as if transfigured, prognosticating that tomorrow he will die and be required to make an account to God (3.10). In this scene and that which follows, the words "larga cuenta que dar de tiempo largo" allude to the many sins ascribed to Jorge and the eternity in which he may atone for them. Unlike Don Juan in *El burlador de Sevilla*, Jorge repents in time to gain entrance to Heaven. The process by which one obtains salvation is paraphrased in the following words:

> *no perdáis punto, porque en solo un punto*
> *ganaréis si lloráis contrito y tierno,*
> *punto en que va a gozar de Dios eterno.*   (3.11)

Images of God and Christ are abundant. Christ is "Monarca eterna" (1.1), "eterno bienhechor" (3.1), and "Varón de dolores" (1.10). Although Christians endure many hardships, they also brighten many lives. This antithetical idea is delicately expressed by Christ: "quien imitarme procura / busque espinas, deje flores" (1.10). God's altar is a "tálamo santo" (1.1), and His home is "soberano Alcázar" (2.4) or a place "donde reina un Dios cordero" (2.8). His justice is inescapable, for every person's deeds are duly recorded in His account book. Jorge paraphrases this idea in a double metonymy, "la justica de Dios es libro y pluma" (3.12).

The Cross on which Christ died is presented in multi-metaphorical form.

> *La cruz tiene Dios clavado,*
> *que es su tálamo, su cama,*
> *su catedra, su palenque,*
> *su esposa, su enamorada.*   (3.15)

In remembrance of the Cross, Juana flagellates herself on another cross,

as a mirror of Christ's ordeal. This action leads her to contrast her state
with Christ's in a series of antitheses in the form of a rhetorical question
that concludes with a chiasmus.

> ¿Yo el pecado, Vos la gracia;
> yo en regalos, Vos en cruz;
> Vos con tormentos, yo sana?   (3.15)

The purpose of earthly existence is to gain God's favor and the assurance of a heavenly eternity. Christ instructs Juana that belief in His
sacrificial death ("cruz") and a display of an humble spirit are the only
way to gain a place in heaven ("silla"). Employing two metonymies,
Christ says,

> Para llegar a esta silla
> tienes de entrar por la puerta
> desta Cruz, que no está abierta
> sino para el que se humilla.   (1.10)

Life on earth is transitory, and Juana reminds Mari that it is foolish
to risk eternal damnation for fleeting pleasures. Her rhetorical question
implies an affirmative response.

> ¿Es buena tomar a censo
> pena eterna, fuego inmenso,
> por el deleite que dura
> la que la sombra y la flor?   (2.3)

The words "sombra" and "flor" represent brevity of life, for both van-
ish in a short time. Life is best spent serving God and His creatures,
with charity toward the poor being especially praiseworthy. In the following lines delivered by Crespo, the "mar" is life and the "naves" are
the poor.

> en este mar los llama naves
> en que la caridad despacha al Cielo
> riquezas de que tiene Dios las llaves.   (2.9)

Although Jorge and the assistant superior are active antagonists in
La Santa Juana: Part II, the opening scene is a scorching attack on Mar-
tin Luther. The emotional epithets aimed at him include "lobo en oveja

disfrazado," "Anticristo austral," "apóstata falso," and "vil Lutero" (1.1). Looking to the Bible (Revelation 13:1), the guardian angel excoriates the Saxon as "dragón terrible / de siete cabezas." When Carlos V arrives, he adds his condemnation.

> que el áspid he de pisar
> y el basilisco y quitar
> del mundo este monstruo horrendo.   (1.1)

Both the asp and the horrible monster are metaphorical allusions to Luther.

It would be difficult to find another dramatic work that surpasses *La Santa Juana: Part II* in its use of physical devices to create religious pageantry. The setting calls for elevated platforms, four niches to the rear of the stage, and numerous instances in which characters fly through the air. In the first act Juana and San Laurel soar to three niches containing: 1)Cortez, with the world at his feet, converted "al yugo de la cruz"; 2)Alonso de Albuquerque, towering over his Christian conquest in Asia; and 3) Felipe II, at whose feet lie the two worlds of Europe and America which he will lead to Christianity (1.1). In the fourth niche above is a tree laden with rosaries. Before revealing the tree, the angel explains that it contradicts Luther's evil and indicates the extension of Catholicism to Ireland. All four scenes presented in these niches are visual expressions of Christianity's expansion.

Arriving on the eve of Juana's confrontation with the jealous *vicaria*, Christ appears on an elevated platform with the Cross on His shoulders and a crown of thorns on His brow. At His side is a throne, upon which rests a golden crown (1.10). The dialogue reveals that the throne and crown symbolize the glory that awaits the Christian after death: "que esta corona de gloria / cuesta corona de espinas."

Christ's final appearance in His crucified form (3.17) is set on an elevated platform. He slowly descends to the main stage, while Juana ascends to meet Him. They meet midway and wordlessly embrace. As they part, Juana remains suspended in midair with her body now bearing the imprint of Christ's wounds—her "joyas." In a seeming paradox, Jesus moves to leave as He tells her, "Contigo quedo" (3.18). The intent of this scene is to represent physically the eternal spiritual companionship that invisibly binds Christian to Christ.

Juana's Christlike nature is demonstrated when she appears on a cross, wearing a coarse robe, a crown of thorns, and a cord around her neck (1.17). By enduring severe flagellations, she hopes to unite her spirit with that of God. Juana always appears to enjoy God's favor, even though her earthly situation is unpleasant. The removal of her veil is an external symbol of her loss of favor with the Church (2.5), but there is never any indication that God is displeased with her.

Scenic devices visually reinforce Mari Pascuala's spiritual reform. At first, she feels that suicide is the method of escape from her sinful surroundings. When a rope is thrown down as if from heaven, she interprets it as God's confirmation of the idea.

> *¿Qué es esto? ¡Ay de mi! Una soga*
> *me arrojaron desde arriba.*
> *¡Que por tan cruel salario*
> *halle el mundo quien le sirva!*   (2.14)

Her plans are thwarted, however, when Juana flies from above, reminding her that "Quien perdonó a Magdalena / te perdonará, María" (2.15). Her words allude to Jesus' forgiveness of Mary Magdalene when others considered her beyond redemption. By linking the two women in this way, Juana implies that salvation is possible. Juana presents Mari with a rosary as a physical symbol of hope and leaves the young penitent to contemplate the force of Christianity in her life.

Saint Francis appears once in response to Juana's prayers. He is on a cross also, with an attending seraphim nearby (3.16). Within *Santa Juana: Part II*, three people appear on a cross: Christ, Saint Francis, and Juana. In this order they range from the divine to the human, each giving ultimate demonstration of their love by means of the cross.

To externalize Juana's direct spiritual communication with her guardian angel, Tirso presents the celestial figure in corporal form. The six separate occasions in which Saint Laurel enters, giving physical and vocal representation to a normally silent and invisible relationship, are found in act 1, scenes 1, 2, 9, and 14; act 2, scene 4; and act 3, scene 2.

Although song does not play a prominent role in *La Santa Juana: Part II*, it is used on two occasions to intensify the religious climate. When the new commander arrives, the villagers laud him with heroic metaphors of biblical inspiration. He is a Holofernes and a Solomon whose vigilant and wise leadership will be a glory to God (1.5). The style of the song is simple to reflect the simplicity of their faith; two singers exchange laudatory verses in stichometric fashion and the chorus sings its approval.

The next time a song appears, it is adorned by musical accompaniment. While celebrating Holy Week the villagers enter singing "Trébole danle al niño, / trébole, ¡ay Jesús, qué olor!" (1.18). In their musical tribute to the Christ Child, the clover symbolizes the Trinity, an idea that the chorus reinforces as it responds eight times with "Trébole" to the soloist's joyful expressions. The entire scene is an image of spiritual and physical well-being, although the actual lyrics are free of images.

A general view of the second part of the *Santa Juana* trilogy reveals a work that is burgeoning with religious images. Since the play deals with the most active part of Juana's career, the abundance of images is quite appropriate.

La Santa Juana: Part III

The third part of *La Santa Juana* is concerned with the saint's last years when she was restored to the position of superior and generally respected as God's chosen one. The action in play revolves around the escapades of Luis, a character who is also of great literary interest. One of Tirso's early Don Juan creations, who foreshadows the Don Juan of *El burlador de Sevilla*, Luis lives a life that is far from exemplary, even though he spent his early years under the tutelage of Santa Juana. His father, Don Diego, often seeks comfort and advice about his son from Santa Juana.

The first two acts of the play center on Don Luis's escapades. He has captivated the heart of the beautiful Inés. Don Diego, knowing that Inés has promised to marry César, tries to convince his son of the impossibility of the situation. Luis seems to agree, and the father, blinded by love for his only child, suspects nothing. Later he even agrees to have César jailed for a night as a kind of practical joke. The father does not know that on the arranged night, Luis will enter Inés's bedroom and compromise her honor. When Don Diego subsequently becomes aware of his complicity in the plot, he delivers a scorching, moralizing tirade. Luis's response is to push the old man down, kick him, and then leave.

Up to this point, Santa Juana has appeared only briefly. However, the last act turns more to the spiritual, and Santa Juana moves to the forefront. Her guardian angel arrives, revealing that death is near. He also bears a gift from Jesus—the Holy Sacrament. On her deathbed, she sanctions Inés's marriage to Luis and obtains pardon for his past acts from César and Don Diego. Almost instantaneously, Jesus arrives seeking His bride. He escorts her heavenward as the admiring nuns and villagers witness her ascension.

Whereas the religious images are restrained in act 1, the imagery gains force in the second act in the scenes when Juana communicates with San Laurel, Jesus, and the Virgin. The last act is almost exclusively concerned with the death of the saintly Franciscan nun. Imagery of religious intent prevails in this section as an effort is made to integrate the earthly story with the heavenly one.

Since the first two *comedias* in the trilogy completely characterize Juana, there are fewer images concerning her in the third play. To the nuns and villagers alike, she is "nuestro amparo, nuestra Santa" (3.19). Luis, the impetuous scoundrel, resents the nun's interference and suspects that she is a special instrument sent from Hell to torment him (1.11).

Indeed, he thinks it is "lisonjera / llamarla santa cuando sobra monja" (2.3). Don Diego disagrees, for to him her very signature reveals spiritual grace and abundance that even John the Baptist would confirm (2.3). Lillo, the comic servant who appears throughout the trilogy, perhaps gives the most realistic description of her when he says, "con ser humana, / la divinidad es mucha" (2.8).

Always revealing humility of spirit in her activities and words, Juana tells the villagers, "Nada valgo y poco puedo" (1.14) when they ask for her intercession. Later Diego gives a more praiseworthy opinion when he says her councils are "espejos / de la claridad de Dios" (3.13). In truth, the nun approaches a Christlike image. Jorge, the antagonist turned penitent, appears before Juana in the midst of his sufferings in Purgatory. Although sympathetic and deeply moved, she laments that she cannot alleviate his suffering.

> *que yo por darte remedio*
> *estas penas padeciera.*
> *¡Si hallar pudiera algún remedio!*   (2.6)

There could be no closer analogy to Christ than this, for Christ assumed the suffering of all humanity, and Juana, in a minor position, seeks to assume the suffering of her friend. As his soul writhes in Purgatory, Jorge still hopes for the reward of Heaven: "que entre las llamas mayores / es céfiro la esperanza" (2.6). Assuming that the flames can be extinguished with water, Jorge begs Juana, "recrea mis secos labios / con agua de tu oración" (2.6). These lines are analagous to Christ's suffering on the Cross and His request for water. The word "agua," moreover, brings to mind the life-giving water promised by Christ (John 4:10) as a symbol of cleansing salvation. Juana begs Christ to pardon Jorge and remove him from the flames. In a well-planned simile she describes the ordeal in terms of metal being purified. His soul is

> entre llamas apurando,
> como metal rico y fino,
> los quilates de aquel oro
> que en vuestra mesa ha de estar.   (2.15)

Juana also intercedes on Luis's behalf. In an oxymoron, his intercessor informs the Heavenly Son that Luis is "un muerto vivo: / muerto en vicios vino al mundo," but she adds that it is possible for him to be "Saulo segundo" (2.15). Jesus replies that pardon will be granted. Luis will no longer resemble the belligerent Saul; he will become "Cual otro Saulo" (2.15). This scene alludes to Saul, the unbeliever, who was converted to Paul, the believer.[7]

Luis is also compared to other biblical characters. Crespo calls him a Judas Iscariot because of his traitorous actions to César, Inés, and his own father, and because, like Judas, he attacked his father (3.2). Judas attacked Jesus, the physical form of God the Father, whereas Luis physically attacks his earthly father and rejects his spiritual one.

César looks to the story of Cain and Abel (Genesis 4:1-16) and finds an analogy between himself and Luis. He is a Cain who would like to slay Abel (Luis), but remembering Cain's harsh punishment for Abel's murder, César determines to hold his anger in check and let God seek vengeance on his behalf. In the following lines, sword is synonymous with anger as César speaks,

> que está mi espada envainada,
> mejor vengaré mi ofensa

---

[7]Acts 9:1-20, 13:9.

> *estando contra él la espada*
> *de Dios alzada y suspensa.* (3.5)

Both are fragile and are easily broken. With her words, Juana conveys
the idea that humans are naturally weak and apt to sin.

> *vidrio es todo;*
> *quiébranse del mismo modo*
> *los vasos nuevos y viejos.* (2.8)

On the other hand, God and His Son are perfect. The essence of God is
love: "Es todo amor Dios" (3.13). His home is heaven, and He is "dueño
de aquesa gloria" (2.6). God's Son, Jesus, the Christ, is beyond description for Juana. When she beholds Him, her metaphors of praise are generous and elaborate.

> *Eterno amante,*
> *David, Salomón, Asuero,*
> *Hombre de Dios, león, cordero,*
> *pastor, Rey, niño, gigante.* (2.15)

Through the guardian angel, Jesus sends Juana three gifts which are
symbolic of His love: the Cross, the nails, and the Holy Sacrament. To
her, these are jewels whose splendor exceeds that of the stars. In hyperbolic metaphors she declares,

> *¡Oh, qué prendas manifiestas*
> *tengo, madres, del amor*
> *de mi divino Señor!*
> *¡Oh, qué joya tengo entrellas*
> *que aventaja a las estrellas*
> *en belleza y resplendor!* (3.9)

Similarly, Christ's wounds are precious to Juana, for she sees them as a
"fuente divina" that offers spiritual experience, hope, health, and regeneration (1.6).

The Virgin and the guardian angel are the only other celestial figures
who are paraphrased poetically. The Holy Mother is lauded in terms of
nature's glory.

> *Virgin amorosa,*
> *luna, sol, palma en Cadés,*

plátano, cedro, ciprés,
lirio, clavellina, rosa. (2.15)

The guardian angel is greeted by Juana as "guardadamas" of her house, and then, in a clever simile, she compares him to a salamander: "fénix de amor que se abrasa / como salamandra en él" (1.13). Salamanders were thought to endure fire without harm, and San Laurel's flame of love is equally indestructible. He recognizes Santa Juana's devotion and declares himself her "guardajoyas," signifying that he will keep her heavenly treasures until she can collect them in Paradise (1.13). In his role as custodian, San Laurel is called God's "page de guarda" (2.6).

A predominant theme in this final play of the *Santa Juana* trilogy is the idea that life is only an introduction to eternal existence that begins with death. Soliloquizing, Juana observes that life should be viewed as a battle against evil, and for the victor, the reward is heaven: "todo ha de ser pelear / que al fin se canta la gloria" (2.14). In the same scene she admits that when the body becomes tired, it sometimes may be tempted to abandon the rigorous life. She asks herself if she wants to be like the sons of Ephraim who chose to turn back in fear, rather than accompany Gideon to the victory.[8] The analogy to the weak in faith is odious to her noble spirit, and she pushes her body to the victory (death and union with God). She then proceeds to form a chiaroscuro figure in which life is day and death is night. Day is short; therefore, one needs to be diligent in work (good deeds). Life is a day's work, and at its conclusion appropriate wages will be paid.

en el día de la vida
ha de ganar el jornal
que en la noche de la muerte,
como el jornalero, cobra. (2.14)

Night is not a sinister figure in this interpretation; it merely marks the end of one part of life and the beginning of another. It is threatening only for those who have not lived in a manner acceptable to God. Those who have taken bread (partaken of the Sacrament) are told that they will not have done it in vain: "no os digan después / que tomáis el pan de balde" (2.14). Heaven will be theirs.

---

[8]Judges 7:3

Juana sees her own earthly existence as a "destierro pesado" that separates her from her Divine Husband (2.15). If life is painful exile for Juana, death is a welcomed relief. When Christ asks if she wants to return to Heaven with Him, she joyously consents, if it will be "para no volver" (2.15). She is asking for the permanency of death rather than an ecstatic interlude. Later, Jesus responds affirmatively, causing the nun to react with an emotional outburst of images praising death (3.6). It is an introduction to "eterna paz, a enamorada vida, / al néctar de su vista deleitoso." The winter has passed (life on Earth) and the tender months of April and May (life in Heaven) are beginning. Juana's raptures cause the guardian angel to reappear, and in his company, death becomes even more attractive. It will be a release from the prison created by Adam's original sin.

> rotos los grillos del pesado hierro
> que Adán echó a los hombres de tal suerte,
> que no hay romperlos otro que la muerte.   (3.7)

San Laurel echoes her joy in a circumspect paranomasia, "subes / pasando estrellas y pisando nubes" (3.7).

Easter Sunday is the day chosen for the ascent of the saintly Franciscan. The holy day is paraphrased by the angel in the following lines:

> La Invención sacrosanta,
> mañana, de la Cruz celebra y canta
> todo el mundo.   (3.7)

This day will be "fiesta," and Juana hails Jesus' nails and thorny crown as "galas de mi fiesta" (3.9). The instruments of the Crucifixion open the door for believers, and with them, Juana confidently, joyously awaits death. In true Christian form she voices the optimistic paradox of a death that gives spiritual life, "parto mañana / a la patria de la vida" (3.9).

Heaven is also paraphrased in traditional images. It is the "tálamo amoroso" of her Divine Lover, a city "donde el bien mora," a royal palace or a tranquil house "donde no llega el mal ni el bien se pasa" (3.6). In the presence of the angel, Juana speaks of the "patria soberano," and he, of "Sión bella" (3.7). In the last scene Christ invites His chosen one to the "Palacio eterno" (3.22).

The production of the third part of *La Santa Juana* is less elaborate than the second, but superhuman acts still prevail as external displays of spiritual movement. The first of these symbolic appearances occurs when Christ arrives in a scarlet robe (symbolic of His blood) as if risen from the dead (1.7). He is elevated, as is Juana beside Him, to show their ethereal natures and close union. Christ then causes the Cross to appear, adorned with a crown of thorns, and three nails. He explains the significance of each. He places the crown on Juana's head saying, "Esta corona de espinas / sembró en mi cabeza amor." Next the Cross is placed in her right hand as "noble prenda." Finally she receives the three nails, "estos que a mis esclavos / libraron." Juana is being prepared for a Christian death in this stylized scene that represents spiritual ecstasy. When Christ leaves, the ecstatic nun descends to the ground to meet her guardian angel (1.8). In other words, the ecstasy is over, and an earthbound soul is left with the guardian angel as her only method of communication with Jesus.

In the second act, Tirso reintroduces Jorge, a central figure from Part II. Juana prays for his soul and asks to know if he is in Purgatory. No sooner is her question formed than a large bronze bull appears, breathing fire (2.5). Since interpretation of this omen is difficult, divine aid arrives in the form of the guardian angel. Juana's eyes are opened to see the bull's gaping side, which reveals Don Jorge writhing in flames (2.6). It is now apparent that this is a visual representation of a soul in Purgatory.

Purgatory is actualized again when one of Luis's friends visits him. He is shown to have a physical form, but in reality he is a soul suffering purification in Purgatory. Flames issue from his hands and he tells Luis, "este fuego labra / nueva vida," meaning that he will be cleansed sufficiently to enter Heaven. When Luis reaches out for his friend's hand, he feels the heat transferred first to his hand and then it is as if his entire soul is consumed by the flames. This is Tirso's way of giving visualization to the tortures of Purgatory and the possible salvation it contains for its inhabitants. In addition, the transference of the flame to Luis serves as a physical warning of a spiritual condition.

Juana's physical levitations were often shown in Part II, but in this play she soars through the air on only one occasion. As she flies toward Ana Manrique, Jorge's ailing widow, one of the nuns spies her. This metaphysical elevation prompts the admiring witness to say,

Goce yo dese trofeo;
alguna prenda procuro
cual de Elías a Eliseo;
arroje, siquiera, el velo,
si Elías arrojó el manto.   (2.7)

The reference is to the incident in the Bible in which Elijah parted the
water with his mantle, while Elisha witnessed it (1 Kings 2:6). The analogy points to Juana as Elijah and the young nun as Elisha.

As Juana grows closer to God and death, her spiritual senses are
sharpened. The audience is impressed with this fact by the physical appearance of the Virgin, Jesus, San Laurel, and another angel (2.15). The
simultaneous confrontation by so many divine creatures is further evidence of her purification. By her deeds, Juana merits the company of the
Holy Family. The purpose of this scene is to foreshadow her death.

In the last act, a jewelry box appears on a table. It contains Juana's
jewels—the Cross, crown, and nails that Christ gave her, as well as another jewel that she has yet to see (3.9). The box is opened and, amidst
golden clouds, the *Santísimo Sacramento* emerges. This is the "prenda"
(3.7) or "joya" (3.9) promised by Christ. The chest is easily seen as the
Body of the Church, protecting the symbols of Christ's sacrifice. This
particular sacrament will be Juana's final Eucharist feast and a prelude
to eternal life and Christ's body which will be shared in Heaven. She calls
the symbolic bread "celestial hartura; / maná de eterna dulzura" and
"medalla de amor galán (3.9). Keeping in mind the Catholic belief that
the Eucharist bread actually becomes Christ's body, the personified images of the bread take on increased significance.

Fin de mis enojos,
pan de leche, pan con ojos,
....
mañana os comulgaré
y la gloria alcanzaré
pues llevo en Vos la libranza.   (3.10)

The last three scenes are the most elaborately produced in the third
part of *La Santa Juana*. They concern Santa Juana's actual death, in an
atmosphere permeated with a heavenly aura. To the rear of the stage, a
curtain draws to reveal Santa Juana kneeling with the Cross and crown
of thorns. The nuns are gathered at her side, completing the religious

tableau (3.20). As death nears, Juana raises her hands in prayer while the sisters continue to kneel in humility and adoration (3.21). The moment death is accomplished, Christ appears on the stage (3.22). He takes His bride by the hand and leads her up a platform. As they mount toward heaven, the guardian angel says, "Aquesta corona y silla / es para la Santa Juana." Although the stage directions do not indicate the presence of a royal throne, it is assumed that this one exists in mental imagery. Considered from the aspect of imagery, these concluding scenes are a visual representation of the movement of a purified spirit at the moment of death.

LA NINFA DEL CIELO, CONDESA BANDOLERA Y OBLIGACIONES DE HONOR

La Ninfa del Cielo (1613) is a drama that artistically blends secular and religious elements. The first two *jornadas* revolve around a love triangle, while the third moves into the realm of theology. Tirso's two moral lessons were directed toward defining humanity's responsibility and pointing the way to salvation. The play's concluding lines indicate that the subject matter is based on fact.

> *Y aquí*
> *da fin* La Ninfa del Cielo,
> *cuya prodigiosa vida*
> *por caso admirable y nuevo,*
> *Ludovicio Blosio escribe*
> *en sus* Morales ejemplos.   (3.18)

A study of Blosio's works reveals neither a personage by the name of Ninfa nor one whose life resembles that of Tirso's heroine. For this reason, there is much divergence of opinion as to the true identity of the title character. Karl Vossler logically assumes that Blosio supplied the basic plan of showing God's mercy toward sinners and that the plot was a product of Tirso's original genius.[9] Blanca de los Ríos carefully came to the conclusion that *La Ninfa del Cielo* is an exclusive creation of Tirso's that expresses the two dominant forces within his soul—the hagio-

---

[9]Karl Vossler, *Lecciones sobre Tirso de Molina* (Madrid: Taurus, 1965) 74.

graphic element and the pagan poetry of the Renaissance.[10] Whatever his sources were, the result is a work of artistic merit. Of interest is the fact that this drama was the fount of inspiration for Tirso's *La Ninfa del Cielo* (*auto*).[11]

The title character, Ninfa, Condesa de Valdeflor, is a beautiful Diana-like character, who spends her life hunting and enjoying the glories of nature. Into this setting enters Carlos, a handsome noble, with whom she promptly falls in love. Unknown to her, Carlos is married to the daughter of the king of Naples. After robbing Ninfa of her heart and her honor, Carlos secretly returns to his wife. The effect on Ninfa is dramatic: she gathers a band of warriors and declares war on the male species. Together they roam the mountains, killing countless men and inspiring fear in all.

Meanwhile, Carlos discovers that he has fallen in love with Ninfa and returns to declare his love. Instead of a sweetheart, he faces a vengeful warrior who demands that he slay his wife to prove his constancy. Before this can be accomplished, Ninfa has a vision of death that leads her to seek forgiveness for her rash, inhuman acts. She discards her warrior's armor and dons the robe of a penitent. She even rejects Carlos. When her transformation is complete, Carlos's wife arrives, seeking her husband. Ironically, she is the instrument of Ninfa's death. The duchess sees a movement in the bushes and, thinking it is an animal, lets an arrow fly. In a spirit of Christian forgiveness, the wounded Ninfa pardons her executioner and begs Carlos to find joy in God. The last scene shows her going to a pedestal where Christ awaits, thus indicating a union of souls in typical mystic terms.

Nearly all of the religious images of *La Ninfa del Cielo* are contained in the third act; however, preferences for these images over those of a worldly nature can be noticed at the end of the second act. The numerous images characterizing Ninfa are of a religious nature. In her warlike attitude, she boasts of being "pública bandolera / del Cielo" (2.12). An angel admonishes her, "Deja el ser ninfa del mar / que has de ser ninfa del Cielo" (3.16). In these two antithetical metaphors that introduce the drama's title, there is an indication that the pagan nymph will move to-

---

[10]Blanca de los Ríos, 1:912.

[11]Ibid.

ward a heavenly image. When a spiritual crisis causes Ninfa to examine her present life, she excoriates herself in a series of metaphors.

> *Soy una esclava*
> *del demonio, una mujer*
> *la mayor y la más mala*
> *pecadora que ha tenido*
> *la tierra entre todas cuantas*
> *ha sustentado y sustenta.*
> *Soy, al fin, Ninfa.*   (3.4)

Ninfa becomes humble after her soul has felt the fire of God's love. In a poetic simile she compares herself to a wounded deer and God to the thirst-slaking water.

> *y como de amor me habéis*
> *herido, Señor, el alma,*
> *herida y llena de fuego*
> *vengo, como cierva al agua.*   (3.3)

The basis for this image is borrowed from Psalms 42:1: "As the hart panteth after the water brooks, so panteth my soul after thee, O God." The same image of "cierva" is carried over into the last act when the duchess mistakes Ninfa for a deer (3.16).

Still ecstatic from her unique religious experience, Ninfa is jolted back to reality by the appearance of Carlos. By means of contrasting images, she explains that her spiritual union with God prohibits any relationship she might have had with him: "que ya soy de Dios esposa, / y tuya no puedo ser" (3.15). Next she attempts to explain the duality of her nature. Her body has sinned against her soul. In repentance, she constantly flagellates herself with a chain. The chain is of double significance; besides being overt self-recrimination for human error, it is a reminder that the body chains the soul to earth and away from God. The image of the repentant flesh is artistically paraphrased in the following lines:

> *hecho pedazos el pecho,*
> *sangriento el cuerpo y llagado,*
> *porque con esta cadena*
> *que arrastro por tierra en pena,*

y prisión de mi pecado,
justamente le castigo
toda la noche y el día,
que ha sido del alma mía
mi más mortal enemigo.   (3.15)

The third act, bearing great resemblance to the religious *autos*, traces the movements of Ninfa's soul towards purification and attempts to define her relationship with God. Images are in great abundance, both visually and aurally. In a soul-searching soliloquy, Ninfa calls upon God as "Esposo amado," "mi bien," and "gloria de mi vida" (3.13). She continues lyrically describing the parts of His body in terms she turns into metaphorical images.

Es a la parda avellana
semejante su cabello;
al blanco marfil su cuello;
sus mejillas, a la grana;
su frente es nevada falda,
que de mil claveles rojos
termina un valle; sus ojos
son dos soles de esmeralda;
corona las niñas bellas
de celajes carmesíes;
sus labios llueven rubíes;
sus dientes nievan estrellas.   (3.13)

Images of sin, repentance, and atonement overlap with regularity in *La Ninfa del Cielo*. Frightened by a fleeting view of death, Ninfa is moved to mend her sinful ways, which she declares in an alliterative simile.

Como culebra quiero
para otra vida nueva renovarme
donde clemencia espero.   (3.1)[12]

Progressing toward greater spiritual awareness, the sorrowing young woman tells the hermit Anselmo that the cruel suffering of Hell can scarcely compensate for her crimes on earth (3.4). On a subsequent oc-

---

[12]Tirso uses this same image in *El condenado por el desconfiado*, act 2, scene 18.

casion, Ninfa is moved to tears as she ponders her unworthiness. "Ninfa soy / de las fuentes de mis ojos," (3.13) she moans, giving hyperbolic measures to the abundant tears of contrition she sheds. Christ does forgive her, and as the drama draws to a conclusion, the child of God looks forward to death. "Es buscar a Dios, que aquesto / es regalo para mí," (3.18) she tells Carlos in a Christian paraphrase of death.

When death finally claims Ninfa, she interprets it as God's vengeance: "quien a hierro mata es justo / que muera también a hierro" (3.16). In the form of a modified chiasmus, her words paraphrase the Old Testament philosophy of an eye for an eye, a tooth for a tooth.

From the middle of the second act onward, Tirso shows a decided preference for allegorical scenes. The first occurs when Pompey's wife appears onstage. One of Ninfa's warriors, Pompey, hanged his wife to prove his complete allegiance to Ninfa. The cruelty of his act horrifies Ninfa, however, and she sentences him to death. Meanwhile, the wife is rescued. With the executioner's rope still around her neck, she intercedes on behalf of her husband: "aunque es mi enemigo / es mi marido, en efeto" (2.8). This scene can be interpreted as a mirror of Christ's life. Pompey's wife returns as if from the dead and offers forgiveness to her husband who, in a moment of blindness, betrayed her. The close analogy to Judas' betrayal is apparent, and on a broader level it could include Christ's pardon of all sinful people who seek redemption.

The main allegory is initiated in the last three scenes of the second act when Ninfa is pursued by the king's soldiers. Exhausted from the chase, she finds shelter in the mountains, where she drifts off to sleep and has a sequence of dreams in the form of the dance of death. One by one the dancers fall into the deep pit (2.15). As Ninfa approaches its rim, Death materializes and tries to converse with her. Ninfa's suspicions that this is the pit of death are confirmed (2.16), and her logical conclusion is that death is inescapable. Since she appears to the be next victim, Ninfa decides to hasten her fate by plunging into the pit before Death can claim her. As she is poised to leap, an angel appears saying,

> *Ninfa, no te desesperes,*
> *que no has de serlo del mar,*
> *que más hermoso lugar*
> *te han dedicado.*   (2.17)

The "mar" represents her damnation and loss of God, and the contrasting "más hermoso lugar" indicates Heaven. The angel then identifies himself in words that are a paraphrase of a guardian angel.

> Un amigo, el más amigo
> que en tus sucesos tú viste;
> que desde que tú naciste
> ha andado siempre contigo.   (2.17)

Ninfa accepts her guardian in good faith, and the act concludes with her spiritual regeneration as "Ninfa del Cielo." The entire dream sequence is an allegory of Ninfa's struggle within herself to find meaning in life. The forces of evil have drawn her close to Hell's gate, but God's promise of salvation brings new hope and life.

Ninfa's penitent soul is exhibited in another allegory. Carlos hears chains rattling from offstage, which he prefers to ignore. The sound gradually increases until a bedraggled creature enters, dragging a heavy chain and carrying a skull in her left hand. In her right hand, she carries a rock with which she scrapes her breast. Carlos's servant Roberto is the first to recognize the penitent Ninfa (3.5). Her physical sufferings mirror the emotional tortures of her soul.

Ninfa had received the instruments of her penitence from Anselmo, the hermit who advised her to cross the river and begin a new life (3.6). In her efforts to reach the other side of the river, she accepts a ride with a strange boatman. As Ninfa begs for mercy, the sinister guide tells her, "¡Muere, ingrata, / que el mismo a quien serviste, ése te mata!" (3.9). There is no doubt that this is a paraphrastic allusion to Satan. The allegory is apparent: the opposite riverbank represents a new life, guided by Christ. The river is the line that separates the evil from the good life. The boatman who plies his trade in the water is a composite figure representing the temptations of evil that threaten one's safe arrival to godliness. Ninfa is rescued from a watery death by a custodian who demands her safe delivery (3.10). His role is that of a saviour, or perhaps a guardian angel.

Christ makes two appearances—both intended to externalize the spiritual communication between God and Ninfa. He first appears briefly as a shadowy reflection in a fountain (3.14). When a timid Ninfa dares to look in the water, Jesus speaks to her.

> Ninfa mía, en esta fuente
> te dejaré mi retrato,

> *aunque es imposible estar*
> *ausente de nado Yo.*   (3.14)

With these words He vanishes, leaving Ninfa to ponder their import. The reflection of Christ, hinted at but never actually seen onstage, suggests the invisible spiritual element. The image of water, used earlier to indicate evil (2.17), now becomes a symbol of purity, with the fount alluding to the life-giving water of Christian knowledge and to the baptismal waters. The brevity of the scene (only nineteen lines) illustrates the suddenness with which Christ can reveal himself to the human soul.

The following scene continues the image of water with a reverse intent. Ninfa gazes into the fountain, still overcome by her encounter with Christ. She is suddenly shocked and frightened to see Carlos's face reflected there. In an antithetical observation, she contrasts the divine and the diabolical forces that have wrought dramatic change in her life.

> *Pues donde el Cielo me honró,*
> *del perro que me mordió*
> *el retrato miró en ti.*   (3.15)

The spiritual and scenic climax of *La Ninfa del Cielo* occurs when Christ comes to claim His bride. In this ecstatic moment, Ninfa declares her complete surrender to God's spirit in a traditional Christian image: "por vuestro costado quiero / entrarme en Vos" (3.18). The synecdoche "vuestro costado" represents Jesus, whereas "Vos" in this context signifies that she accepts the belief that Jesus and God are one and that only through Jesus can she receive salvation.

While Christ is descending from an elevated platform, Ninfa is ascending toward Him. Death is definitive when the two meet on an equal level. Ninfa delivers her spirit to Jesus, and immediately the curtain covers the alcove in which this action took place. The abrupt dropping of the curtain gives an impression that the audience has been permitted a brief glimpse into Ninfa's soul. The physical evidence is quickly abandoned, and that which lingers is the memory of the "santo cuerpo," whose soul ascended heavenward to live eternally with Christ (3.18).

In addition to the scenic effects in the allegorical segments of this drama, there are other occasions when visual elements impress ideas. Costuming is symbolic for Ninfa. Dressed in warrior's paraphernalia, she represents a sinful, murdering bandit—an enemy of Man and God. When her encounter with death opens her eyes to her possible future, she removes every vestige of her warlike occupation and hangs her arms, helmet, and armor on the branches of a tree (3.1). The visual effect of these trappings so displayed, contrasted to the simple raiment worn by Ninfa, dramatizes her spiritual regeneration.

As her soul is increasingly moved to seek God's favor, Ninfa assumes the role of a penitent. She wears a hair shirt and a penitent's robe, and drags a heavy chain. The chain symbolizes the sins that have dragged her down and which now make difficult (but not impossible) her approach to righteousness.

The hermit Anselmo also takes on a visual role. When Ninfa discovers him outside his hermit's hut, he is clothed in leaves and carries a lantern in his hand. The lamp might be interpreted as a glimmer of light that his holiness offers to a sorrowing soul. Anselmo is a reflection of God's spirit; it is he who offers her hope of salvation as he gives voice to the play's title.

> *que la mano soberana*
> *de Dios quiere hacerle Ninfa*
> *del Cielo.*   (3.4)

La Ninfa del Cielo is one of Tirso's most praiseworthy dramatic works. The plot is logically developed, the messages clearly presented, the poetry superb, and the scenery well integrated with dialogue. Ninfa can be taken as a model of any erring soul striving toward perfection, and in this sense the entire drama is universal in content.

SANTO Y SASTRE

Tirso based the hagiographic work *Santo y sastre* (1614-1615) on the life of San Homobono, a twelfth-century tailor and cloth merchant of Cremona, Italy.[13] The details of his life are followed rather closely, although his wife, Dorotea, is painted in a somewhat more sympathetic manner than church records indicate. As the title suggests, the play revolves around the life of one person whose activities prove that it is possible to be both a businessman and servant of the Lord.

---

[13]Blanca de los Ríos, 3:49.

The action begins as Dorotea, a wealthy, young girl, tries to decide whether she should marry Lelio or Grimaldo, but even as she is discussing the situation, a mysterious voice echoes that her choice will be a tailor. Later that day, when Homo Bono, a young tailor, arrives to measure her for a gown, Dorotea instantly falls in love with him, in spite of his pedantic, moralizing nature. He flees in terror, but Dorotea's money is quite attractive to Homo Bono's family. They convince him that he would be insane to turn his back on such an opportunity. Reluctantly he agrees to the marriage, after being assured that he can continue his extensive charitable activities.

As the months pass the little tailor's days and nights become so filled with charitable occupations that there is scarcely enough money to feed his immediate household. God miraculously supplies this need, but Dorotea becomes more and more disgruntled as the forgotten wife. At the peak of her discontent, Lelio determines to claim Dorotea for himself, but before they can escape, God intervenes to thwart the plan. In a spirit of divine forgiveness, Homo Bono pardons his enemy and prays for his regeneration. Both Dorotea and Lelio are convinced of the tailor's holiness, and now they have only words of praise for him. In the last scene, it is learned that Homo Bono resides in Heaven where he is clothed in the glory of God.

The simplicity of the plot contrasts with the complexity of the poetic style. Images of a religious nature are abundant and at times extended in their forms. The title *Santo y sastre* is an antithetical paradox used to describe concisely one who combines a lowly profession with spiritual nobility. Pendón, the gracioso, thinks that this combination is as divergent as "blanco y negro, fuego y frío" (1.1). When he adds, "mal podrá volar un sastre," the implication is that a lowly tailor could never expect to soar spiritually.

Pendón is rather obsessed by the idea of saint and tailor, and in an effort to reduce the spiritual state to concrete terms, he makes recourse to earthly objects combined in clever oxymorons.

> *¿sastre y santo? ¡Cosa rara!*
> *Cuervo blanco, nieve negra,*
> *luz oscura, firme paja,*
> *sol de noche, poeta rico,*
> *caballero sin mohatras,*

> *viuda de noche y sin duende*
> *doncella no pellizcada,*
> ....
> *es decir que hay sastre y santo.*   (1.4)

Pendón's attitude toward the tailoring profession moves from scorn to admiration, until he finally declares himself Homo Bono's apprentice. Eulogistically he discusses the etymology of the word "sastre." God represents three in one, and when the tailors appeared before God in search of a name, He dubbed them "San Tres," because they supplied clothing of skins after Adam and Eve disobeyed God ("quebrantó el ayuno").

> *no sastres, sino san tres;*
> *porque el Santo tres y uno*
> *cortó a nuestros padres fieles*
> *vestidos de aquellas pieles*
> *cuando quebrantó el ayuno.*   (2.5)

Tirso employs a variety of images in his presentation of the central figure, Homo Bono. The name itself is symbolic of a saintly person, and as time passes, nearly everyone agrees that he merits it. Dorotea's opinion wavers from admiration to scorn and finally to unquestioning loyalty. On meeting him, she sees him more as a *cura* than a tailor. She says, "Sastre Santo, vos vestís / almas, que los cuerpos no" (1.3). When he spurns her, she attacks him for his insincerity: "santo sólo en las palabras; / aquél que virtudes vende" (1.4). When he subsequently accepts her as his bride, Dorotea affirms his saintliness: "no es deste mundo" (2.3). Her admiration culminates when she says, "¿no es él un pino de oro? / pues la virtud es su esmalte" (2.4).

Homo Bono is not always endowed with a large amount of modesty. When a jealous Lelio burns his house, the long-suffering tailor announces that he will accept this misfortune as calmly as did Job. Fire cannot destroy his soul; hence, he will not despair (2.11). Again referring to the ravages of the fire, he explains that these earthly goods are only on loan from God. He is a "jornalero" and "rentero" of God's land (3.1); therefore, he has no right to complain. Conversely, the tailor chastises his wife for complaining about the deprivations brought about by his charitable acts, likening her to Job's querulous wife (3.1).

The third act is almost entirely spiritually motivated. In one scene Homo Bono is at his sewing table when a voice sings to him of the crucified Jesus. This leads the pious tailor to contrast his comfortable condition with Christ's suffering, by means of rhetorical questions.

> *¿Vos en Cruz y yo asentado?*
> *¿Vos muerto por mí y yo vivo?*
> *¿Yo sano y Vos doloroso?*
> *¿Vos desnudo y yo vestido?*   (3.5)

He concludes this series of moving antitheses with a simple oxymoron that pleads for Christ's redeeming grace: "¡Ay pobre rico, / vestidme Vos agora de Vos mismo!" Within the scene, the refrain is repeated six times, first by the mysterious voice that could represent the tailor's conscience or soul, and then by Homo Bono. Three times the exchange is made—in imitation of two-part harmony. The effect is one of humility, contrition, and unworthiness. The use of the verb "vestidme" also incorporates the vocabulary of the tailor on a divine level. Homo Bono's sincere feeling of his own unworthiness is rewarded by a vision of Christ. He is overcome at the sight and cries,

> *Vístase, amoroso amante,*
> *el hombre torpe y lascivo*
> *sedas que el gusano teja;*
> *que yo dichoso me visto*
> *desta humilde desnudez.*   (3.6)

Here there is a contrast between earthly vanity and Christian humility that longs only for the robe of God's grace. The last two lines are paradoxical when they suggest that the tailor might dress himself in nudity. On a spiritual level, nudity is synonymous with purity and innocence.

Homo Bono is also compared to John the Baptist. An interpretation of John's sacrifice in terms of the tailor's trade implies that Homo Bono's acts are comparable to the martyr's. All acts that please God contribute to making clothes for the God-Christ who ended His life on Earth crucified and bereft of clothing. Nudity, therefore, takes on a dual role in this consideration. Not only was Christ physically nude, He was also stripped of human love as He was put to death. From that day on, all charitable acts performed by Christians are viewed as efforts to return love to Christ and to reclothe Him spiritually. The ensuing poetic image describes the Apostles' efforts:

> *Desnudo os ve, y pues le rompe*
> *el dolor de su martirio*
> *las telas del corazón*
> *de tela podrá vestiros.*   (3.6)

Christ appears briefly after Homo Bono generously gives his wedding suit to a poor beggar. The clothes were in essence God's, and Christ comes to repay Homo Bono. To show His approval, Christ says, "la ropa que me has cortado / al talle de mis deseos" (2.8). He adds, "bien sabes tomar medidas," signifying that Homo Bono knows how to lead a truly Christian life. In this scene the clothing is also a concrete image of the tradesman's virtuous actions. The height of praise comes when Christ declares,

> *pues justamente me veo*
> *vestido y galán por ti,*
> *y así desde hoy más te tengo*
> *por mi sastre.*   (2.8)

The last scenes form a type of epilogue, informing the audience of Homo Bono's ultimate fate. "Aquel sastre / de la Cámara de Dios" (3.13) ended his days on earth. His death is freedom "de la mortal cárcel / del cuerpo" (3.13) and an opportunity to enter Paradise. The heavenly home is paraphrased thusly:

> *en aquel paraje*
> *donde arenas son estrellas,*
> *donde no llegan combates*
> *del mar, que anega virtudes,*
> *siendo vicios huracanes.*   (3.13)

Throughout the play, spiritual concepts are expressed in terms of the tailoring profession. There are also several occasions when the procedure is reversed, with tailoring terms interpreted on a spiritual level. When Dorotea requests a dress of "verdemar" color, Homo Bono replies that "verdemar" is the image of one's life: "verde" because one is like a green plant that quickly dies, and "mar" because the world is a vast ocean in which one is tossed about (1.2). Dorotea then moves on to dis-

cuss the trimming ("pasamanos") for her gown. The devout servant of
the Lord retorts with an undisputed Christian truism.

> los pasamanos mejores
> son en ellas el Rosario:
> que si las manos le pasan
> de pasamanos podrán
> servir al alma, pues dan
> Pasaporte al Cielo.   (1.3)

The profusion of words formed on the verb "pasar" constitutes a polyp-
toton, although the main thought is contained in the ambiguity resulting
from the dilogy of "pasamanos."

Clothing, when transferred to Heaven, takes on a celestial image.
Heavenly robes are always cut to perfection, for God is the one who
shapes Man's spiritual mantle of glory.

> Es la ropa perdurable
> de la gloria que Dios viste
> sin peligro que se rasque.   (3.14)

Metaphors referring to Christ are "Humanado verbo" (2.7), "dulce
amor mío," and "Pelícano de mi amor, / sol eclipsado divino" (2.6). Jesus' wounds are alternately seen as symbols of hope, consolation, and
asylum.

> de mis esperanzas nido,
> de mis congojas consuelo,
> de mis temores asilo.   (3.6)

In prayer, the tailor addresses the Son with a series of metaphors.

> Mi Dios, mi Señor, mi bien,
> mi Rey, mi Pastor, Cordero,
> mi rico pobre, mi luz.   (2.9)

In the same prayer, Mary is mentioned as "Emperatriz" of the angels because she gave human form to God. To indicate the birth, Homo Bono
reminds Christ that Mary "os vistió del sayal nuestro." The "sayal nuestro" is an appropriate tailor's image for human life.

Adopting a tone that is reminiscent of that found in the Book of
Psalms, a mysterious voice lauds God as Creator of the earth: "los
montes y valles / vestís de hierbas y lirios" (3.6). The voice then describes Mary's grief in concrete terms. By means of catachresis, the song
presents an image of the Virgin's tears which form a mantle for her Son.

> *pues los hilos*
> *de su llanto os tejerán*
> *la tela de sus suspiros.*   (3.6)

Within *Santo y sastre* there are many direct references to biblical
characters and events. When Homo Bono's food chest is miraculously
filled with bread (an event that brings to mind Christ's miracle of the
fishes and loaves), Pendón praises the chest ("arca") as a holy object,
making use of a rather heavy-handed pun.

> *y ella es Arquisinogoga;*
> *arcadas de nuestra fe*
> *que el hambre libra de arcadas,*
> *duquesa de Arcas.*   (3.4)

Pendón thinks it might be another Noah's ark, but then he denies it by
means of a pun on "sí" and "no." With these words he attempts to heap
praises on the miraculous event: "¿de Noé? No dije bien / de *sí* he" (3.4).
Homo Bono considers the implication of the occurrence and discusses it
in terms of the business world. Good deeds are repaid by God at prime
interest (life in Heaven). The miracle of the bread is only a foreshadowing of heavenly reward: "que fue dar muestras del paño / con que nos
viste en la gloria" (3.4). Note the return to the tailor imagery in these
lines—passing from "pan" to "paño."

On one occasion a jar of water is turned into wine (3.3). To Dorotea,
it is a mirror of "el milagro de la boda / de Caná de Galilea" (3.4). Each
incident (the biblical one as well as the one in Homo Bono's life) represents protection for those of complete faith.

The image of Zacharias is invoked as the tailor prays for Lelio's recovery (3.9). His words are an enactment of intercessory prayer. As
Homo Bono begs compassion for the mute sinner, he assures Christ that
henceforth Lelio's lips will sing praises as sincerely as the priest Zachar-

ias pronounced the *Benedictus*.[14] "Cantará después de mudo / del modo que Zacarías," intones Homo Bono; his words will comprise a "Himno de la iglesia eterno" (3.9).

Tirso is not extremely complimentary to women and marriage in *Santo y sastre*. Looking to religion, he forms disparaging images. Pendón observes that marriage is a "religión estrecha," to which Homo Bono rejoins that it is "tanta carga a cuestas" (2.2). The word "cuestas" evokes a vision of the Cross, which Pendón readily adopts, forming an image of a religious procession. The tailor is the penitent who suffers the cross of marriage, while Pendón assumes the role of light bearer.

> *Como quien lleva la cruz*
> *de matrimonio excelente,*
> *tú serás el penitente*
> *y yo el cofrade de luz.*   (2.2)

The conversation concludes as the gracioso cynically insinuates that woman is a creature to be feared—why even God waited until Adam was asleep before He created Eve!

In a more serious vein are two images inspired by the sacrament of the Eucharist. The first is contained in a song, expressed in the language of the tailor. It praises Christ as a synthesis of the Godhead and human blood—a finely woven brocade, whose glory will be celebrated in a new mass (Eucharist). The voice creates an aura of splendor as it sings,

> *El oro de sus cabellos*
> *esmalta el rosicler fino*
> *de vuestra preciosa sangre*
> *para que valga infinito;*
> *decid, pues son de brocado,*
> *que os teja ornamentos finos,*
> *celebraréis Misa nueva.*   (3.6)

The second image is linked to Homo Bono's death. Valerio reports that one of the tailor's last earthly acts was partaking of the Eucharist sacrament. It is described as:

---

[14]Luke 1:5-64 relates that Zacharias was struck dumb by the Lord, but his speech was subsequently restored, causing him to sing praises to God.

> *Aquel sacrificio*
> *misterioso y inefable*
> *en que obliga el sacerdote*
> *que al pan Dios del Cielo baje.*　　(3.13)

Santo y sastre does not employ lavish staging, but on several occasions, low key scenic activity reinforces religious concepts. As Homo Bono establishes his identity as a pious tailor, he produces a tape measure. This small prop opens the door for a complex figure. The tape is a divine mystery, according to the tailor, because it is made of "piel de un cordero muerto" (1.3). Implied is Christ, the Holy Lamb, though he does not make the analogy clear until a few lines later when he comments,

> *Mida pues el pergamino*
> *las ropas, y si es cordero,*
> *Cristo lo fue verdadero*
> *ya humano, si antes divino.*　　(1.3)

In one scene, Homo Bono removes his fine wedding clothes and gives them to a beggar. He explains that this is an effort to emulate Christ. Christ, the bridegroom of the Church, approached the wedding completely unadorned, except for His crown of thorns. By removing his finery, the pious tailor hopes to approach his own worldly wedding with simplicity and purity. He explains the act in terms that are not too flattering to his bride.

> *esposo soy,*
> *Cruz me ponen, y así quiero*
> *en mi Cruz estar desnudo*
> *por imitarle hasta en esto.*　　(2.7)

In the next scene, with a background of appropriate music, a tableau is presented on an elevated rear platform. The beggar, dressed in his newly acquired finery, appears, bearing a resemblance to Christ. He speaks in the manner of Christ, reinforcing the idea that an act of charity to a lowly brother is an act of charity toward God (2.8). This vision of Christ-in-Man and Man-in-Christ vanishes, and Homo Bono is left alone feeling almost ecstatic. As he prays to Christ, his spiritual closeness with Him is visually reinforced. Beginning the prayer kneeling humbly, he becomes completely absorbed in the Spirit, and as he remains in a kneeling position, a stage device slowly raises him heavenward (2.9).

Beginning with the third act, more activity is aimed at intensifying the religious atmosphere. Homo Bono is now portrayed as a semi-Christlike figure, who has virtually rejected all worldly hindrances. He is confident that God will protect him and his home. From offstage a voice assures him, "No temas, ve tú a mi casa, / que Yo guardaré tuya" (3.2). Obviously this is God instructing Homo Bono to continue his Christian service.

In a succeeding scene, the tailor appears alone on the stage (3.6). He is seated on a bench while he sews for one of his clients. From within a voice sings of the crucified Christ, contrasting the "trajes profanos" of earth with Christ's celestial robe. In prose, Homo Bono responds to the song. There are three verses to the song and three responses. The intent is to show a man as a prosaic creature and, then, by introducing the unseen voice (which must be Homo Bono's soul speaking), his spiritual side is revealed. As the scene develops, the tempo increases, and the tailor is swept under the influence of the spirit. At the spiritual climax, Christ descends from above the stage, slowly approaching Homo Bono. Simultaneously, the tailor climbs toward Christ—totally unaware of his movement. About midway, the two meet and embrace wordlessly. No explanation is needed to clarify their action as a representation of the ecstatic union of two souls. The request contained in the song's refrain, "Vestidme agora de Vos mismo" (3.6), has been granted.

The most spectacular stage effect in the entire play is in response to Lelio's attempt to enter Dorotea's home. As he kicks open the door, an angel appears on the threshold with a flaming sword. Lelio is so overcome that he falls into a faint as the angel strikes him dumb (3.7). This is an externalization of God's protective spirit and an affirmation of His promise to protect Homo Bono's home. The image is strongly suggestive of the angels placed at the Garden of Eden to bar human entry.

In the last scene (3.14) the spiritual and earthly elements are combined. Onstage, Pendón, Dorotea, and Lelio speak of the roles they will play in life now that Homo Bono is dead. At the same time, to the rear of the stage, an alcove is unveiled, revealing San Homo Bono dressed in a long robe. In his left hand he holds a pair of scissors and in his right, a cross. Celestial-type music creates an image of Paradise as the faithful soul slowly rises toward Heaven. Homo Bono's general appearance here may not be in the best of taste, but the image clearly indicates a soul who combined the physical with the spiritual while on earth. The "Santo y sastre" now ascends to his reward. In this scene, the placement of the action is most important. At the center of the stage the worldly action takes place and, at first glance, is predominant. To the rear of the stage and elevated above the earthly characters, a small platform presents the real message and captures the audience's attention. The scene represents the meaning of life, illustrating that worldly activities capture human attention, while a broader, spiritual world is waiting in the background to give meaning to existence. This is the recurrent message in *Santo y sastre*.

CHAPTER III

THE BIBLICAL PLAYS

E arly in his dramatic career, Tirso de Molina recognized that the Bible contained a wealth of material that could be adapted to stage productions. In the ten years between 1611 and 1621, Tirso produced five plays that were directly inspired by the Bible. Three were pure tragedies: *La mujer que manda en casa* (1611-1612), the story of Jezebel; *La vida y muerte de Herodes* (1612-1615), a psychological study of King Herod Antipas; and *La venganza de Tamar* (1621), a story of incest and murder. *La mejor espigadera* (1614), the story of Ruth, and *Tanto es lo más como lo de menos* (1614), Tirso's most original biblical play which incorporates the parable of the rich miser with that of the prodigal son, conclude on a more optimistic note. All five are faithful reproductions of the Holy Record, with many scenes appearing to be direct paraphrases from the original source. Except for *La vida y muerte de Herodes*, each deals with Old Testament figures and has a woman as key personage.

Within the biblical cycle, a stylistic fluctuation is fairly obvious, although each play is contrived to maintain a religious tone. Where the plot is more profane, religious images are introduced as one means of recapturing the biblical atmosphere; however, in a play whose plot is essentially religious, Tirso did not always feel the need for such imagery, preferring to rely on the innate religiosity of the story itself. An individual analysis of each play will definitively reveal the variety with which Tirso applied religious images.

LA MUJER QUE MANDA EN CASA

Jezebel, the beautiful, idolatrous queen of Israel, is the title character of *La mujer que manda en casa*. Since her flamboyant life and macabre death follow the pattern of pure tragedy, Tirso merely assembled the elements to please his artistic sensibility. Based on the incidents recorded in 1 Kings 16:20-22:37, the play stresses the conflict between the Jehovists and the worshipers of Baal.

The first act establishes Jezebel as a predatory, amoral woman who rules both the country and her husband, King Ahab. She has even convinced Ahab to abandon his religion in favor of Baalism. Fearing for the Israelites, God moves to reclaim Ahab. The prophet Elijah appears, warning that evil will befall all of Israel unless Ahab turns back to God. Ahab turns a deaf ear to the admonitions and instructs his soldiers to kill the prophet. Elijah and his followers flee to the mountains where they remain for three years.

Meanwhile, Ahab covets the rich vineyards that adjoin his property. The owner is a loyal Jehovist, Naboth, husband of Rachel. With unheard of boldness, Naboth refuses his king's offer to buy the vineyards. Jezebel and Ahab, enraged by such an insult, plot to destroy him. Naboth is accused of blasphemy by false witnesses and is stoned to death. Naboth's vineyards are transferred to Ahab, and Baalism appears to be victorious.

Elijah emerges once again to forecast that Ahab and Jezebel will both die for their cruelties and that the dogs will lick the blood of Ahab in the same place they had licked Naboth's. His words are fulfilled. Ahab is killed in battle, and his bloody body is devoured by dogs on the very spot where Naboth was stoned. A short time later, Jezebel falls from the tower of her palace when she attempts to seduce Jehu, God's chosen successor to Ahab. When her body falls to the ground, dogs rush toward it and seal her fate. Jehu speaks with prophetic authority as he offers hope to Israel, and the thesis of Tirso's play is reinforced.

> *Alce Israel la Cabeza,*
> *pues de Jezebel se libra,*

y escarmiente desde hoy más
quien reinare; no permita
que su mujer le gobierne;
pues destruye honras y vidas
La mujer que manda en casa,
como este ejemplo lo affirma.   (3.9)

La mujer que manda en casa contains more religious images, particularly ones that are scenic and allegorical, than any other of Tirso's biblical plays. This is true probably because Jezebel's life was basically profane; without constant reminders of the religious atmosphere that prevailed over the small but fervent group of Jehovists, the play's tone could degenerate to a completely worldly level. The elaborate production contrasts sharply with that of *La mejor espigadera*, a play whose basic inspiration is spiritual, thus eliminating the necessity for the use of religious images to set the tone.

Images of biblical characters occur throughout the play. Jezebel is called "mujer perdida" (1.6), "de Profetas verdaderos / verdugo" (3.13), and "águila ejecutive" (3.16), whereas her rule is metaphorically described as a punishment sent by God: "Dios nos castiga" (1.3). The external beauty of the heathen queen is contrasted with her moral decay when Naboth expresses his surprise that "en tal belleza / pueda caber tan crueldad" (1.7).

Elijah, "el gran Zelador" (3.11), is alternately praised as "luz de santos celadores" and "de Dios justo Profeta," and scorned as one of the "hipócritas taimados" (3.13). His death and ascension to Heaven are paraphrased with the catachresis "En carroza de eternos resplandores / arrebató una nube al del Carmelo" (3.13).

Another biblical character, Moses, is excoriated by Jezebel in a triple metaphor based on Exodus 2:12, 12:37, and 16:31.

> *Ese verdugo de Egito,*
> *que cruel tantos ha muerto,*
> *ése, que por un desierto*
> *llevó número infinito*
> *de hebreos y sin delito,*
> *cuarenta años desterrados*
> *por veniales pecados*
> . . . .
> *Profeta falso Moisén.*   (1.1)

God is also described in the simple metaphors "señor de inmensos nombres" (2.6), "piedad inmensa" (2.12), and "Señor de eternal alteza" (3.13).

Reflections on life and death form philosophical, religious images. In a Jehovist image, Naboth views life as a gift from God: "Toda vida humana es corta; porque a censo se nos dio" (2.10). Believing that earthly acts govern one's fate after death, Naboth rejects Jezebel's adulterous attentions. He sees them as a diabolical force that would bar his entry to Heaven; therefore, he tells her, "túmulo eterno me trazas" (3.7). In an antithetical figure, an unhappy Jezebel acknowledges the duality of human nature: "galas el cuerpo se viste / y el alma lutos secretos" (3.18).

Images of allegorical import are dominant in this play. In a comic allegory, Coriolín sacrifices his burro to supply meat for Elijah and his prophets who are hiding in the mountains. The gracioso cannot understand why this sacrifice is necessary. He loves his burro and feels that his love should be sufficient protection for the animal (2.3). This scene alludes to the Israelites who cannot understand the loss of life through wars and famine. As God's chosen people, they feel that their love of God should grant them immunity from witnessing the dreadful sufferings of their loved ones.

Later, when Ahab asks the devout Naboth to sell his vineyard (2.9), the implication is that he hopes to bribe his neighbor into effecting a union of their two religions, thus diminishing the power of Jehovah.

Following the biblical account (1 Kings 18:22-40), Jehu reports on the test that was to establish either Jehovah or Baal as the true God. Two piles of wood were placed on Mount Carmel. While Elijah, as God's sole representative, prayed for God to ignite his pile of wood, more than four hundred prophets of Baal prayed that their wood would receive fire. God delivered the fire to Elijah, while the Baalists' prayers to their idol went unheeded. The parable-like nature of the account established the supremacy of God and His prophet Elijah over the religion of Baal. Jezebel becomes enraged and, in synecdoches, vows to annihilate the prophet: "¡Yo le beberé la sangre! / ¡Yo pisaré su cabeza!" (2.13).

In a scenic allegory, an angel arrives at Mount Carmel, bearing bread and water for Elijah (3.2). The playwright's intent is to express, through physical symbols, the spiritual sustenance that God provides for the faithful. The bread and water can be interpreted as prelusive symbols of the Christ that God will hand down to future generations as ultimate proof of His love.

A bizarre allegorical scene shows Jezebel forcing Naboth to declare his position (3.6). He is confronted by three plates. One holds a crown wrapped with a cord, symbolizing the royal position that Jezebel will offer him if he will strangle his wife with the cord. The second plate holds a sword and a woman's robe as reminders of Jezebel's dual roles: "Hierro para castigarte / y toca, para quererte." The third plate is covered with stones, suggesting the manner in which Naboth will die if he rejects Jezebel. Naboth contemplates the three plates and successfully manages to transfer the symbols to his own religion.

> *pues tira Jezabel*
> *piedras a Dios, no está cuerda.*
> *Espada de su malicia,*
> *dad al Juez Supremo cuenta,*
> *pues, lasciva y torpe, afrenta*
> *la espada de la justicia.*
> *Corona; si en su cabello*
> *serviste de insignia Real,*
> *bájaos y seréis dogal*
> *con que suspendáis su cuello.*
> *Cordel, servid de escarmiento*
> *a los idolatros vos,*
> *. . . . .*
> *y para dar la respuesta*
> *la vil corona derribo.*   (3.6)

Naboth overturns the crown—an act that constitutes a rejection of Jezebel and her idolatrous religion.

Dreams and songs also take on allegorical implications in this play. Rachel reports that she dreamed of a serpent, bathed in blood, draining the life from her husband. She immediately recognizes the serpent as Jezebel (3.9), thereby interpreting the allegory for the audience. Soon after Naboth's death, Jezebel hears a woman's voice singing of a turtle dove bound by chains (3.16). The dove is lamenting the death of her lover who has been killed by a cruel eagle. After hearing the first verse, Jezebel comments on the allegorical nature of the song: "Me canta y alegoriza / mi crueldad metaforizan." The second verse refers to vineyards, nests, love, and jealousy, which can easily be transferred to incidents in the lives of Rachel, Naboth, and Jezebel. The succeeding verses contain simple metaphors that leave no doubt as to the hidden meaning. Jezebel is the eagle, and Jehu, the newly crowned king of Israel, is "el león coronado." The final lines symbolize Jezebel's downfall.

> *Humillará su soberbia,*
> *caerá el águila atrevida,*
> *siendo presa a los voraces*
> *lebreles que la dividen.* (3.16)

Scenic imagery is elaborate throughout the entire play. The opening scene of the first act presents a tableau with three points of interest. On one side of the stage, Jezebel appears in hunting habit, accompanied by Rachel and a servant. Other hunters with dogs surround her, and hunting horns can be heard offstage. On the other side, a large group of soldiers, including Naboth and Jehu, march onstage to the accompaniment of the warlike sounds of drums and trumpets. To the rear of the stage, Ahab, king of Israel, poses in his royal robes and jeweled crown. The position of the king indicates that his reign spans war and peace, as well as two predominant religions. The effect is that of a colorful pageant.

Dressed in the humble robe of a penitent, Elijah attempts to turn Ahab back to God. Irritated by the prophet's moralizing, he orders his soldiers to kill him (1.10). The attempt by the soldiers to seize Elijah is a visual exposition of Ahab's desire to silence God's voice in the land, whereas Elijah's miraculous escape from the soldiers may be interpreted as God's intervention on behalf of His follower.

While Ahab, Jezebel, and Jehu dine in the garden, a chorus sings that Israel has two suns: "el del Cielo y Jezabel" (2.4). Two soloists attempt to establish which is more powerful—God or Baal. The chorus denies God's supremacy in a chiaroscuro refrain, singing of the repression ("Se eclipsa") of the God of Israel and the rise ("luce") of Jezebel's religion.

> *Eso no, que el dios del Delo*
> *se eclipsa y cubre de un velo,*
> *y el nuestro luce más que él.* (2.4)

In the same scene, a pair of ravens fly into Jezebel's garden and seize the food from her table. By their color, the birds signify unhappiness, and by their actions they indicate that Jezebel will not have complete submission. Ahab curses the omens of bad luck as "aves torpes del infierno," fearing that they presage his death: "plumas de luto me anuncian / el mísero fin que espero" (2.4). The ravens reappear at Elijah's camp, offering their food to the prophet of God (2.6), thus completing the symbolism begun two scenes earlier. The evil ones are deprived, and the godly are supplied by His grace.

Naboth's broken body is presented onstage on a mound of blood-stained rocks (3.11). Doubly significant, the sight symbolizes the persecution of the Hebrews and the power of Jezebel, since it was she who plotted his death. However, the queen's reign is doomed—a fact she recognizes when she looks in a mirror and sees the bloody reflection of Naboth, armed with a knife that is directed toward her (3.17). The scene externalizes the threat that Naboth's death poses for her.

The concluding scene (3.19) is most elaborate. With scepter in hand, Jehu enters with a band of marching soldiers. From another door, Obadiah enters with his large retinue, while Jezebel appears at a balcony. From the midst of the crowd, Jehu and his followers mount a platform onstage, where Rachel crowns him king of Israel. Flageolets, drums, and trumpets augment the majesty of the occasion. Physically, the stage presents the two religious factions that have divided Israel and indicates a future in which a godly king will attempt to reunite the country. This scene is a reversal of the opening scene (1.1) in which Jezebel and Ahab were shown to be more prominent. Also in this scene, Jezebel's macabre death is enacted onstage. Jehu's soldiers seize the evil queen and throw her to the rocks beneath the balcony, where voracious dogs attack her body. As in the death of Ahab, the vengeance of God is accomplished.

LA MEJOR ESPIGADERA

The Old Testament book of Ruth provided the inspiration for *La mejor espigadera*. Tirso adhered closely to the biblical version, although he took the privilege of interpreting the character of Elimelech and inventing his manner of death. Credible but unsubstantiated conditions existing during the famine are interpolated for dramatic effect, as well as an account of a dream predicting the union of Ruth and Boaz. The first two acts are an elaboration of Ruth 1:1-5, while the third contains a more or less factual, albeit dramatic, presentation of the remaining chapters (Ruth 1:6-4:22).

Naomi's husband, Elimelech, is portrayed as a greedy man with a consuming selfish interest. He has chosen to protect his fortune rather than help his countrymen whose lives are being destroyed by the famine in Bethlehem. Greed causes him to move his wife and sons, Mahlon and Chilion, to neighboring Moab where he can better guard his riches. Ironically, shortly after moving there, Elimelech is robbed and killed by a band of Moabites. His distraught family elects to remain in Moab, and eventually the sons marry Moabites. With the passage of time, the sons die, and Naomi is left without means of support. Mahlon's widow, Ruth, refuses to abandon her aging mother-in-law; therefore, when Naomi decides to return to Bethlehem, Ruth accompanies her.

Once in Bethlehem, Ruth resorts to the lowly occupation of gleaning behind the reapers to eke out sustenance for herself and Naomi. In a short time, Boaz, her wealthy kinsman, notices the gentle woman and gives orders that she be treated kindly and that grain be left for her. In Hebrew custom, Ruth seeks protection from her relative, Boaz, and he joyfully accepts her as his wife. The dramatic account of their tender love story concludes with an allusion to the kings that will be born from their lineage in future generations.

The image of God's love is clearly indicated throughout the third act as Ruth and Naomi are joyously welcomed by the inhabitants of Bethlehem. Their neighbors shower them with generous gifts in an overt expression of their love. Charity at its highest point is embodied in Boaz's solicitous concern for the noble young widow. The atmosphere of brotherly love that exists in Bethlehem contrasts sharply with the greed exhibited by Elimelech in the opening scenes of the play. The spirit of love lingers over the entire last act, but its selfless essence is best expressed in Ruth's oft-quoted words to her mother-in-law.

> *viviré donde vivieres;*
> *seguiréte donde fueres,*
> *ya la suerte te persiga,*
> *ya de fortuna mejores.*
> *Tu patria es mi patria ya;*
> *tu ley preceptos me da;*
> *adoraré el Dios que adores.*   (3.3)

Specific religious images occur throughout the play, but they are closely oriented to the biblical account, leaving little room for great originality on Tirso's part. Centered around God, Ruth, and Naomi, most of the images are of a traditional nature. Referring to the gentler side of God's nature, Boaz identifies Him with the metaphors "Colme de bendiciones, / el Señor infinito" (3.10), while Naomi recognizes His sternness, seeing a tangible image of God's anger in the death of her two sons who turned from the Hebrew religion when they married Moabites (2.2).

The vengeful hand of the Lord may be seen in the famine that grips all of Israel, paraphrased as "la ira divina / que nos quiere castigar" (1.1). When Naomi asks God to explain the purpose of the famine, her paradoxical question is based on a dual interpretation of the word "pan." First it refers to the physical sustenance, and in the last line, the spiritually motivated phrase "Casa de pan" is a veiled allusion to Christ's birth.

> *¿Por qué en Belén, Dios de Abraham,*
> *el pan les habéis negado,*
> *si es Belén casa de pan?*   (1.7)

Several religious images take their inspiration from the title character. Although Ruth's actions speak louder than words, Boaz ventures to describe her as "peregrina piadosa," and in another metaphor that makes use of hyperbole, he refers to her concern about Naomi's welfare as "la caridad más nueva / que vieron nuestros siglos" (3.10).

Naomi paraphrases the selfless nature of her daughter-in-law in an explication of the play's title.

> *Jamás su memoria muera,*
> *y el amor, mientras, espiga*
> *pan, con nuevo blasón diga:*
> La Mejor Espigadera.   (3.6)

Ruth's conversion to the Hebrew religion is expressed in a figure that contains metaphors alluding to God as well as to Moses and his law.

> *la ley que cuerda truecas,*
> *por la que el dedo ha escrito,*
> *de Dios, que dio a Moisés*
> *nuestro primer caudillo.*   (3.10)

On several occasions, the central characters of the play are compared to other biblical personages. In three instances, Naomi provides inspiration for these religious images. In speaking of her generous nature, she is likened to Noah (Genesis 9:20) by means of a pun on "Noé" and "Naomí."

> *Basta empezar en Noé*
> *su nombre para ser buena,*
> *que el vino inventó.* (1.2)

Naomi wants to help the starving Israelites, even though her greedy husband forbids it. She remembers that Joseph eased the famine in Egypt (Genesis 41:56) and sees an analogy to her own situation.

> *Si de Egipto el hambre fiera*
> *nuestro José socorrió,*
> *aunque extraña nación era,*
> *y mi casa enriqueció*
> *el Cielo de esta manera,*
> *¿por qué en ella ha de faltar*
> *a los de Israel sustento?* (1.3)

In the next scene, Jabel recalls the deeds of Abraham (Genesis 22:1-20) reflected in the pious acts of Naomi (1.4).

Ruth fell in love with Mahlon the moment she saw him, just as Jacob was immediately attracted to Rachel. The parallel nature of their situations is stated in a simple analogy: "De aquesta suerte sería / Jacob cuando vio a Raquel" (1.10).

Allegorical imagery is introduced only once in this play. In an extended speech, Ruth speaks of a dream that Boaz had, in which a rock, in union with a tree of Judah, produced a mountain that reached as high as God's throne. Seeing the grandeur of the mountain, a sheep left Heaven to graze on its pastures. Boaz's prophets had interpreted the dream in the following manner:

> *del tronco de Judá*
> *el sueño alegre predice*
> *la casa real de Bohoz;*
> *y que la piedra sublime*

> *de quien nacerá la vara*
> *que el más alto Cielo humille,*
> *será una mujer gentil*
> *de Moab, bella y humilde,*
> *que casándose con él,*
> *el cordero amante oblique,*
> *que de los pastos sabrosos,*
> *donde* ab aeterno *reside,*
> *al monte de Judá baje*
> *para que a Dagón derribe.*   (2.6)

The symbolism of the dream is made even more explicit as the sages conclude that Ruth is the stone and Boaz the royal tree. Through their union, a noble mountain (the House of David) is created that nurtures the Lamb of God (Christ).

> *cuyas raíces*
> *el monte pronosticado*
> *producirá en que se críe*
> *El Cordero que Israel*
> *ha tantos siglos que pide.*   (2.6)

Two scenic images visualize religious concepts. In the Hebrew religion, the prospective groom places his cloak over the head of the bride to symbolize that he assumes responsibility of providing shelter and protection: "marido es el abrigo / de la mujer" (3.16). Boaz places his cloak over Ruth's head as acknowledgment of their betrothal (3.16) and as an external symbol of their spiritual union.

Boaz's last words in the play forecast the birth of their son, Obed, first in a line of illustrious descendants.

> *de Obed, Jesé, que fue padre*
> *de David, rey y profeta,*
> *de quien, descendiendo Cristo,*
> *hace la memoria eterna*
> *de Rut.*   (3.19)

At the conclusion of his speech, a curtain is drawn to the rear of the stage, revealing a tree on which the lineage of David, from Jesse to Boaz, appears. With this visual image, the play concludes.

TANTO ES LO MAS COMO LO DE MENOS

Of Tirso de Molina's five biblical plays, *Tanto es lo más como lo de menos* is his most original. He has interwoven the parable of the rich miser (Luke 16:19-31) and that of the prodigal son (Luke 15:11-32) in such a manner that it is almost impossible to conceive of their ever existing in separate forms. Neither parable is weakened, for each shares equally in plot development—a fact that is mirrored in the title and clarified in the last lines of the play. Tirso has altered a few minor facts of the biblical versions and given symbolic names to the characters (Clemente, Felicia, Liberio, Gulín), but the moral lessons are in no way diluted; in fact, they seem to be strengthened. Tirso's style complements that of the Bible, leading one critic to consider this play as the gospel according to Téllez.[1]

Tirso invented the character Felicia to form a link between the two parables. The main characters are Nineucio, a rich miser; Lázaro, his nephew; and Liberio, the prodigal son who longs for his father's death so he can receive his birthright. Each of these men wants to marry Felicia, but Nineucio is the elected groom, since he appears able to provide more happiness immediately. The two younger men, while not poverty stricken, cannot equal Nineucio's wealth.

Bitter over his rejection, Liberio demands his inheritance and flees to Egypt. He lives in splendor until fire destroys his possessions and gambling and extravagant living deplete his fortune. Nineucio arrives, and the prodigal seeks aid from him, only to be cruelly rejected. Lázaro, too, travels to Egypt, where his fortune is quickly dispersed among the less fortunate. Predictably, Nineucio refuses to give food or shelter to his charitable nephew, for the bonds of money are stronger than the bonds of blood. Against the background of Egypt's serious famine, Nineucio's miserliness is even more horrifying.

Felicia almost instantly regrets her choice of Nineucio as a husband. Helpless, she witnesses his cruelties while she prays that she may find escape from the unhappy marriage. At this time, God's hand reaches out to place things in their proper perspective. Nineucio is struck dead when he refuses to aid Lázaro for the second time, and Lázaro, in turn, dies

---

[1]Serge Maurel, *L'Univers dramatique de Tirso de Molina* (Poitiers: L'Université de Poitiers, 1971) 341.

of starvation. Having witnessed the two deaths, Liberio sees the folly of his ways and returns to his home where his father receives him with joy and affection. Felicia is betrothed anew to Liberio, and their future looks bright. Clemente counsels his son to follow a golden mean in his life, being neither too miserly nor too liberal.

> *Vicioso pródigo fuiste,*
> *y aquél, mísero avariento;*
> *tanto en ti fue lo de más,*
> *como en él fue lo de menos.*
> *En medio está la virtud:*
> *si son vicios los extremos,*
> *de Lázaro el medio escoge*
> *y tendrás a Dios por premio.*   (3.21)

The religious images in this play are predominantly used to portray the three main characters—Nineucio, Lázaro, and Liberio. Nineucio's atheism is attested by Liberio as he says, "eres Dios de ti mismo" (1.1) and by the remark, "siendo su dios la gula" (3.1) by the gracioso, Gulín. Nineucio himself alludes to his atheism: "Nacer y morir: no hay más" (2.5). He then proceeds to justify his miserliness because of his atheism, alluding to both conditions by way of paraphrase.

> *mi vientre es mi Dios; ni pido*
> *ni doy: sólo es bien empleado*
> *lo que conmigo he gastado;*
> *lo que con otros perdido.*   (2.6)

The miser's lack of Christian charity is expressed in an alliterative metaphor: "vivo no abrió jamás / piadosas puertas al pecho" (3.20). Early in the play, Nineucio's character is established when he indicates that the poor are the garbage of the world—a fact that he hopes to justify by means of a biblical reference. His words reveal the hardness of his heart.

> *Los pobres y la basura,*
> *echadlos al muladar.*
> *En Job esta verdad fundo,*[2]

---

[2]The entire Book of Job is a lamentation of physical deprivation.

> *pues luego que empobreció,*
> *en un muladar paró,*
> *por ser basura del mundo.*   (1.11)

Lázaro's charitable acts are "agregación de bienes en los Cielos" (1.4). Felicia aphoristically observes that he shall obtain "a costa de la mortal / la felicidad eterna" (1.2). To Lázaro, charity is a gift to God that helps elevate one to the Heavenly Kingdom. In this image, the words "reyes" and "reina" symbolize those who please God by their charitable actions, while "esclavo" is a metaphor for those bound by their miserliness.

> *Hoy paga, hoy tiene que dar,*
> *y el dar es reyes: salga*
> *cuando hace mercedes, reina;*
> *cuando las recibe, esclava.*
> *Da a tus deudos, da a los pobres,*
> *y no serás semejanza*
> *de estéril tierra en invierno.*   (1.12)

Images of Liberio and his actions are abundant. He and his brother Modesto are likened to Absalom and David, respectively, as Liberio says, "Sabio David en ti tengo / cuando ser quiero Absalón" (1.8).[3] In the same scene, Clemente warns his son that he is destroying his own inheritance. On a spiritual level, "hacienda" and "tesoro" indicate Heaven and "perdición" and "ocaso" refer to Hell.

> *y eres por vivir sin rienda,*
> *ladrón de tu misma hacienda,*
> *pirata de tu tesoro.*
> ....
> *tu perdición misma abrazas,*
> *corriendo ciego, a tu ocaso.*   (1.8)

Liberio finally realizes that he must pay for his sins. Alluding to a biblical verse (Galatians 6:8) he says, "que, en fin, todo labrador, / del modo que que siembra, coje" (3.7). His sins are beasts: "Sirvo, por servir mis

---

[3] Whereas Absalom rashly murdered his brother (2 Samuel 13:30-40), his father David was revered for his wisdom (2 Samuel 5:1-5).

vicios / los brutos que los imitan" (3.6). With his eyes now opened to the consequences of his reckless life, Liberio gives a physical description of his spiritual return to God: "¡Mi Dios! dadme Vos la mano; / levantadme, pues caí" (3.9).

The return of the prodigal is an allegorical scene of an erring sinner returning to a loving, forgiving Heavenly Father. The biblical style of Clemente's antithetical words reinforce the intent of the scene.

> Todo sea regocijo,
> pues muerto en vicios resusita un hijo.
> Perdióseme, y ahora
> restituído alegra, porque llora.   (3.18)

Images alluding to Man's spiritual life on earth occur regularly within this play. Modesto initiates the philosophical tone when he observes that life on earth is a river that is all too soon swallowed up by death (the sea).

> que es mar la muerte inclemente,
> y suele sorberse un río
> en mitad de su corriente.   (1.5)

Continuing the image of life as a river, Lázaro views the poor as ships that can transport him to Heaven: "pues sois del cielo navíos, / mi hacienda al cielo llevad" (1.15).

With "piedras" representing Man's sinful acts and "pan" symbolizing Christ, Liberio comments on Man's unworthiness: "dando a Dios piedras por pan" (3.8). Shortly after this he employs double metaphors to accent humanity's basic, sinful nature, addressing the soul as "Alma del Cielo enemiga / . . . hijo de Adán" (3.9). In an extended metaphor, Man's existence as a spiritual creature in a materialistic world is contrasted with that of a tree.

> Arbol se llama al revés
> el hombre, y si en todos ellos
> son raíces sus cabellos,
> y son los ramos sus pies,
> árbol con propiedad es,
> que más perfección encierra;
> mas ¡ay de mí, cuánto yerra

> *quien por gustos de mentira,*
> *raíces que el Cielo mira,*
> *quiere arraigar en la tierra!* (3.3)

Religious ecstasy is paraphrased by gentle Lázaro. The implication is that during moments of ecstasy he has longed for death and the glories ("zafiros") of Heaven. The traditional images "grillos del cuerpo," "pedir treguas," and "espíritu torpe" emphasize the eternal nature of Lázaro's condition.

> *¿Nunca tu espíritu torpe*
> *en éxtasis suspensivos,*
> *ya velando, ya durmiendo,*
> *pidió treguas a los grillos*
> *del cuerpo, breves instantes,*
> *pensamientos discursivos,*
> *remontando por los Cielos*
> *y midiendo sus zafiros?* (1.15)

On two occasions, scenic images are effectively employed. Early in the play, Lázaro and his uncle appear onstage, offering a picture of contrasts. Lázaro and the poor people he aids are on one side of the stage; on the other are posed the elegant Nineucio and his retinue of servants (1.13). After the visual presentation of their characters, the two men engage in a brief conversation that establishes the Christian charity of the former and the grasping miserliness of the latter.

The last scene in the play is a visual interpretation of Tirso's moral thesis. The parables are virtually abandoned as he takes a direct approach to the theological problem. The stage presents two contrasting scenes. Above is a representation of Heaven, showing Lázaro in robes of gold and white, resting in the lap of Abraham. Below, in a minature Hell, a flaming Nineucio is seated at a table laden with dishes. Each dish gives forth flames and the audience is made to believe that the insatiable gluttony (avarice) is constantly fed with flames, thus increasing his tortures. Abraham and Nineucio converse from afar—their physical separation showing the vast gulf between the two spirits. Abraham explains the visual image concisely and poetically.

> *No hay dos glorias, no hay dos Cielos:*
> *él recibe, descansado,*

de sus virtudes el premio;
tú en tormentos perdurables
pagas los males que has hecho.
Mal te podrá socorrer
desde lugar tan diverso
al en que estás, que hay abismos
de inmensa distancia en medio.   (3.21)

The message for all of humankind is apparent. Temporal life is a preparation for eternal life, and one should measure one's actions accordingly.

LA VIDA Y MUERTE DE HERODES

La vida y muerte de Herodes is the only biblical play by Tirso dealing with a New Testament figure. His sources for the plot were Matthew 22 and a five-volume biography of Herod by Flavio Josefo, which was translated into Spanish in the fifteenth century.[4] Material gleaned from Josefo's account supplies the body of the first two acts, while the biblical account of Herod's slaughter of the infants dominates the third act. The rivalry between Herod and his brother Phaesalus and Herod's sacrifice of his own son are undocumented facts that Tirso added for dramatic effect.

In this tragedy, Tirso presents a psychological study of the infamous Herod the Great, which is in part sympathetic, but ultimately denounces him as a monster. As Antipater's second son, Herod is denied the rights of inheritance; therefore, he establishes his fame as a fearless warrior. Returning from a victorious campaign, he learns that his brother is betrothed to the girl he hoped to marry—Mariamne, daughter of King Hyrcanus of Bethlehem. By a ruse, Herod proves his brother unworthy; thus, Mariamne is led to designate Herod as her bridegroom. Not to be outdone, the brother Phaesalus plots to have Herod executed, but the balance quickly turns, allowing Herod to order his brother's death.

When Herod returns to claim Mariamne, he discovers her with his confidant, Josefo. Although her innocence is obvious, Herod is overcome with rage and has both of them executed. The cold-blooded murders of his brother, his wife, and his best friend establish Herod as a near

---

[4]Blanca de los Ríos, 1:1566.

monster capable of all crimes. When the Wise Men appear, seeking the newborn King of the Jews, the unstable Herod retaliates in a brutal manner. He orders the death of all male children in Bethlehem who are under two years of age. He is so obsessed that he even condemns his own infant son. This act of extreme inhumanity is his own destruction; a supernatural force seems to have overcome him. He dies a raving maniac, clutching the bloody corpse of his son and that of a Jewish infant.

Within the play, the characters, their names, the historical references, the setting, and the action combine to give an authentic biblical atmosphere. The first two acts are directed toward the establishment of Herod's character and the presentation of his amorous activities. Although few religious images are found in this part of the play, the biblical tone prevails. The third act moves into the time of the birth of Jesus, allowing Tirso to present sensitive images of the Holy Child's redemptive mission, exposing the poetic creativity of the inspired playwright. The amorous images found in the first two acts, typical of Renaissance poetry, are replaced in the final act by spiritual images whose inspiration lay in the foundations of Christianity.

The title character inspires many religious images. When the sadistic Herod brags of his cruelties to his brother, he dubs himself "un nuevo Caín" (1.3). Much later, he turns to allegory form when he comments on his mass murder of the children of Bethlehem. Metaphorically, the children are tender plants, sprung from Jewish seeds to be harvested by the wicked ruler.

> La parca soy de las vidas:
> cortaré en pámpanos verdes
> los sarmientos que en Juda
> para atormentarme crecen.   (3.17)

On another occasion, Herod assumes the image of a voracious wolf, while he alludes to the children of Bethlehem as gentle lambs, then as tender plants.

> Lobo soy, corderos busco,
> vuestra sangre me sustente;
> espigas sois de David,
> en berza es razón que os siegue;
> racimos sois de Judá.   (3.19)

Finally, the description of Herod's death again implies an analogy to the murderous Cain, with the two infants likened to Abel: "Murió el bárbaro rabiando / y ahogando los dos Abeles" (3.20).

Images centered around Christ are numerous. Herod paraphrases the Christ Child, with the metonymies "cetros" and "Reyes," indicating the lands He will dominate as spiritual king.

> el triunfador del Oriente
> que, naciendo coronado,
> cetros pisa y Reyes vence.   (3.17)

When Herod becomes aware of Christ's royal nature, he reverts to rhetorical questions to discover the identity of his rival. The wordly king refers to the King in triple paraphrases.

> ¿Quién es éste que a una estrella
> manda ser su embajadora?
> ¿Este que con ella avisa
> tres Reyes y cortes hace,
> éste que al punto que nace
> coronas de Oriente pisa?   (3.12)

In the sacrament of the Eucharist, Christ's body is represented by the Holy Bread. Pachón alludes to this as he describes Bethlehem and the Holy Babe in images of bread.

> si es casa de pan Belén
> creo que sois el Dios pan,
> que para nos hartéis
> de la troj del Cielo abaja,
> pues como pan el la paja
> hermoso grano nacéis.   (3.13)

Herod refers to Christ in negative metaphors when he says that He is "de mi frenesí la furia / causa y principio" (3.14). Herod also makes an antithetical allusion to Jesus' death as he gives vent to human rage.

> si una vez sé donde está,
> túmulo suyo será
> en vez de trono su cuna.   (3.12)

In an extended conversational exchange between the shepherds, Christ is alternately alluded to as the king of clubs, spades, hearts, and diamonds. Each tries to justify his metaphor by commenting on the dual interpretations of the words "espada," "oros," "copas," and "bastos."

Tirso. *Pues el Niño, si a vencer*
        viene al mundo y el pecado
        de nuesa flaqueza armado,
        Rey de espadas vendrá a ser.

Pachón. ....
        que si la divinidad
        que encubre es el oro rico
        que disfraza el pellico
        de nuesa mortalidad,
        y es infinita la ley
        del oro de su riqueza,
        según su naturaleza,
        de oros el Niño es Rey.

Fenisa. *Después, cuando se desangre*
        ....
        bañando flores y ropas
        y el cáliz de mi ventura
        beba en copa de amargura,
        será entonces Rey de copas.

Tirso. *Otro manjar le señalo*
        cuando se eclipse la luz
        del sol y sobre la Cruz
        el triunfo le entre del palo.
        Que si allá su Reino muda,
        y con tal basto deshace
        las culpas, contra quien nace
        Rey de bastos es, sin duda.   (3.15)

Two other verbal images are worthy of note. The first is a eulogy to the Virgin Mary, consisting of a series of metaphors.

    Esa es la luna,
    el sol, el alba, el ciprés,
    la flor, la palma en Cadés,
    la Fenix que sola es una.   (3.13)

In the second image, the Madonna and Child are described as the dawn and the sun in an image designed to reflect the glory of the heavenly pair. Use of the words "gold," "crystal," and "mother-of-pearl" suggest the aura of translucence that surrounds them.

> *y guidos al portal*
> *venturoso de Belén,*
> *aquel brinco de Dios ven*
> *de oro, nácar y cristal,*
> *en los brazos del aurora*
> *que tal bello sol encierra.*   (3.14)

On only one occasion in the play is scenery used to create a religious image. In the latter part of the third act, a small niche is unveiled, revealing the Wise Men kneeling before the Christ Child. The pageant is described by Fenisa in appropriate religious metaphors.

> *Hermosa apariencia a fe*
> *y de fe a lo que imagino*
> *que este aparador divino*
> *por misterio le tendré.*   (3.15)

LA VENGANZA DE TAMAR

La venganza de Tamar is a biblical tragedy based on 2 Samuel 13. The play has a single plot that logically develops toward an unmistakably tragic denouement. No secondary plots intervene, as the style of a *comedia* often dictates, and humor is virtually absent. The story is woven around two episodes in the lives of three of King David's children. Amnon, a strangely brooding young man, is overcome by an incestuous love for his sister, Tamar. By means of a ruse he lures the girl into his room, where he overpowers her. Once his desire has been satisfied, Amnon casts Tamar out and curses her as a sinful instrument. The dishonored, bewildered girl seeks vengeance from her father, but his great love for Amnon blinds him. Since the king refuses to punish his son, Tamar retires to the country where she lives as a shepherdess. Meanwhile, Absalom, Amnon's brother, has vowed to avenge his sister's disgrace. His opportunity arises two years later when he invites Amnon and two other brothers to come to his country home for a visit. By a prearranged plan, Amnon is assassinated while seated at the banquet table. David arrives to discover Amnon's bloodstained body sprawled on the table. Though Tamar claims the murder is a just payment for her dishonor, David's overwhelming grief dominates the closing scenes.

The theme of retribution or vengeance is constantly dominant in the crucial third act of *La venganza de Tamar*. The first two acts set the stage, put the characters into action, and lead the antagonist (Amnon) to commit his crime. The last act sees the avenger (Absalom) move steadily toward his prey. He is inspired by a desire to avenge his sister, but he is also selfishly motivated to annihilate his elder brother so that he may inherit his father's kingdom. Emphasis is placed on the terrible consequences of Amnon's profane love; hence, although the majority of the poetic images are on a worldly plane, there are enough religious images employed to reinforce the basic biblical inspiration of the story.

An image of God emerges when Amnon observes that the Psalms of David are inferior to God's, for "es Dios la musa perfecta" (1.1). Much later, Tamar indirectly alludes to God with a metonymy as she describes her prayer to Heaven as "Suspiros al cielo" (3.4).

Religious images comparing characters to biblical personages or places are numerous. When Amnon hears Tamar singing, he is so overcome by the beauty of her voice that he cries, "Pardios, que lo habéis cantado / como un gigante Golías!" (1.5). Tamar is also referred to by means of a derogatory biblical metaphor, for when she is discarded by Amnon, he scourges her as "fruta de Sodoma horrible" (3.2).

On another occasion, Tamar directs her father, King David, to seek vengeance in the style of Abraham. Note the chiasmus of the last two lines.

> *Ea, sangre generosa*
> *de Abraham: si su valor*
> *contra el inocente hijo*
> *el cuchillo levantó,*
> *uno tuvo, muchos tienes;*
> *inocente fue, Amnon no;*
> *a Dios sirvió asi Abraham,*
> *ansi servirás a Dios.*   (3.4)

When David urges Absalom to forgive his brother Amnon, he tells him to emulate the kindness of Abel, rather then the vindictiveness of Cain.

> *Tu fueras el fénix de él*
> *si estas cosas olvidarás,*
> *y al príncipe perdonarás,*
> *no vil Caín, sino Abel.*   (3.8)

Viewing Amnon's inert body, David sees a similarity between his circumstances and Jacob's, for Joseph, Jacob's son, was betrayed by his brothers just as Amnon was. David cries out his anguish in the following simile:

> *Mas ¡ay! que es sangre heredada*
> *de quien a su hermano mismo*
> *vendió, y llorará David*
> *como Jacob, en sabiendo*
> *si a Josef mató la envidia.*   (3.18)

There are two instances in which religious images are used to allude to the wars against pagan or non-Hebrew tribes. The first occurs when Absalom intimates that God bestows His blessings on such wars: "la guerra que jubila la sacerdocio" (3.2). In the same scene he refers to the religious wars and the heathen enemy with synecdoches: "mi acero incircuncisa sangre esmalta."

The economy of religious images in this play is noteworthy; however, the religious tone prevails, primarily because of its extreme fidelity to the biblical record.

CHAPTER IV

THE HISTORIC-RELIGIOUS PLAYS

Tirso de Molina, like most erudite scholars of his time, was intensely interested in the history of his native Spain. Since religion had always been a dominant force in the land, he became familiar with much of his country's heritage in the course of his theological training. He also spent several years traveling in both Spain and Portugal, during which time he absorbed more of the spiritual and folkloric nature of his people. The Mercedarian's historic propensity is evident in his theatrical works, for it is the exception to find a play in Tirso's collection that contains no reference to Spanish history.

By successfully augmenting the religious element with material inspired by the people and events of the Iberian Peninsula, the historic-religious plays break the restrictive bonds of the hagiographic works. In many cases, these plays deal with the persons who contributed to the growth of the Catholic church, but the temporal aspect is not ignored, as was the case in the hagiographic plays. This study will analyze the religious images contained in four of Tirso's historic-religious plays: *El Caballero de Gracia*, a work that combines religion and politics on a relatively equal plane; *Doña Beatriz de Silva*, a play that initially accents the profane, although the hagiographic aspect later emerges; *La romera de Santiago*, a profane story presented against the background of Santiago de Compostelo, the site of the shrine to Spain's patron saint; and *Las quinas de Portugal*, a play inspired by the formation of that country's Christian monarchy.

EL CABALLERO DE GRACIA

One year after the death of the centenarian Jacobo de Gratis (1517-1619), Tirso de Molina presented a dramatized account of his life in *El Caballero de Gracia* (1620). The play concerns the pious life of the Italian ascetic who transferred his residence to Madrid, where he directed his energies to the founding of convents, hospitals, and churches. Today his memory is kept alive in the capital city by the street that bears his name and by the institutions that owe their existence to his efforts.[1]

Tirso elected to present the portion of Jacobo's life in which he definitively established himself as a man of God, refusing to allow materialism to interfere with his spiritual development. As the play begins, Jacobo's family urges him to marry Sabina, sister of his brother-in-law, Lamberto. Sabina, who loves Conrado, rejects the unwilling, exceedingly pious Jacobo. Subsequently, Jacobo is named secretary to the cardinal of San Marcelo. Immediately the cardinal arranges posts in Rome for Lamberto and Conrado; however, once there they prove their falseness. Both are jailed by ecclesiastical officers. Lamberto manages to escape, and an Italian count offers to free Conrado if Sabina will compromise her honor. Jacobo, now called El Caballero de Gracia, arrives in time to protect Sabina, free Conrado, and pardon Lamberto, while the Italian count, properly abashed, attempts to atone for his actions by donating a large sum of money to the Church.

The Caballero de Gracia returns to Madrid, where his piety and diligent works to further God's kingdom soon lead Princess Juana to appoint him her personal chaplain. As further evidence of his devotion, Jacobo transfers his personal fortune to the princess to aid in the construction of another convent.

In recounting the life of Jacobo de Gratis, Tirso employed an abundance of poetic images that served to accentuate the religious nature of

---

[1]Blanca de los Ríos, 3:261.

the story; however, the bulk of those images are centered around the title character. Several times he is referred to as a saint—by Sabina (1.4), by Conrado (1.10), and by an artist (3.10). An unfortunate captain also refers to his saintly nature, describing his charitable acts with synecdoches.

> Aquestos labios cristianos
> con el socorro en las manos,
> con el consejo en la boca,
> remedio de mi desgracia.   (3.8)

Lamberto is uncertain about his choice of metaphors, declaring that Jacobo's extremely pious actions classify him as either a hypocrite or a saint (1.11).

Jacobo assumes the appellation Caballero de Gracia after he has been robbed and is subsequently rescued and clothed by a man of the Church. The grace of God saved him; therefore, his servant Ricote suggests the appropriate name, Caballero de Gracia (1.9).

After Jacobo convinces himself that it would not be presumptuous to accept the position of royal chaplain, he pledges to build another monastery for a minor order. While the construction takes place, he offers shelter to the unhoused clergy, thus finding personal and spiritual edification. He draws an analogy between himself and Obediah when he says, "Gozaré la bendición / que Dios echó a Obedón" (3.8).[2] Surrounded by clergy, he hopes to absorb some of their perfection and become a better clergyman himself.

In his office as chaplain, Jacobo considers the paradox of a sinner holding a holy office. "¡Sacerdote / un pecador de crímenes cargado!" (3.7), he exclaims. He is especially cognizant of his lowliness when he is called upon to administer the sacraments. He humbly wonders if his boldness will not be punished by God, just as Uzziah was. The analogy is briefly stated in two rhetorical questions in which the sacraments are symbolized by "Dios."

> ¿De Oza no temo riguroso azote?
> Si muere, porque el arca toca osado,
> ¿he de tocar a Dios?   (3.7)

---

[2]Obediah sheltered and fed 150 priests during the famine in Samaria. See 1 Kings 18:3-5.

The religious significance of the sacraments as tangible evidence of God is echoed in the words of the Caballero de Gracia, "tome el cielo en las manos" (3.24). Because of their symbolic nature, he hesitates to accept the responsibility for their administration, feeling that the sinfulness of his soul may in some way tarnish God.

Descriptions of the Spanish king, Phillip II, compare the monarch with one of Israel's great rulers. Juana refers to her brother as a Solomon of Spain (3.1), and Jacobo agrees, "Bien te llaman Salomón / en la justicia" (3.3). The analogy is reinforced when the princess observes that Phillip is responsible for the construction of the Escorial, a monument comparable to Solomon's great temple of Jerusalem (3.2).

Princess Juana and the Caballero de Gracia select a site near the court at the Puerta del Sol for a projected convent. Unfortunately, that location is already occupied by a house of prostitution that enjoys the patronage and sanction of the court. The power of the Caballero de Gracia, however, is not to be underestimated. He exerts his energies toward condemning the house and, after overcoming formidable barriers, is successful. The results are stated metaphorically: "desterré al demonio y puse / celdas, iglesia y campana" (3.2).

On several occasions, the Caballero de Gracia takes on the image of Christ, giving an allegorical slant to the play. When Jacobo's robbers are apprehended, he benevolently forgives them (1.12). Similarly, Conrado and Lamberto are pardoned, despite their treason toward him (2.13). In each instance, the forgiveness appears to be of a divine nature.

Man's ingratitude to the Saviour is presented allegorically in the story of the destitute military officer. The captain begs money from Jacobo (3.8), squanders it, and returns for more (3.20). When Jacobo reveals that he no longer has any personal wealth with which to aid his friend, the captain becomes almost violent. In like manner, Man, content to accept gifts from God, is always ready to condemn Him if all requests are not granted immediately.

Tirso employed a scenic allegory to introduce considerations about Jacobo's post as chaplain. An artist arrives bearing two pictures. One shows Mary kissing the footprints of a priest; the other presents Christ washing the feet of Judas. From the content of the two paintings, Jacobo concludes that this is God's way of saying that he should reject the position: "hace el Cielo un pincel lengua" (3.10). The next scene counter-acts this interpretation, for it presents a conversation between two nobles concerning the election of a president of Castile. They observe that the job calls for one with superhuman powers, but since that is not feasible, a well-qualified man must serve. Their conclusion is thrice repeated in the paraphrase "si un ángel no lo ha de ser / forzoso es el sello un hombre" (3.11). Transferring the principles to his own circumstances, the Caballero relents and accepts the position as royal chaplain.

Ricote's relationship with the maid, Inés, is somewhat allegorical and comically reflects his master's relationship with Sabina. The physical aspect of marriage appeals to him, but at every turn incidents seem to beckon him toward the religious life. Wine reminds him of baptism; when he takes an evening stroll, he invariably meets a priest; and when he dreams, it is of priests. In view of these events, the gracioso renounces marriage, interpreting the omens as an invitation to the pious life (3.12). Inés does not accept this decision easily; therefore, she constantly places temptation in his path. The resolute Ricote views the situation on a spiritual level, seeing himself as a fish rising to the bait. The devil is represented by the fisherman and Inés is the bait.

> Si a la Red de San Luis
> vivimos y en una red
> pesca el demonio por uso
> tanto perdido mancebo,
> ¿qué se espanta si por cebo
> una merluza me puso?   (3.19)

Ricote's spiritual decision is displayed when he appears onstage dressed in the robes of a minor cleric. With a pun on the word "cuerno," he explains the significance of his dress: "Este es un traje esquinado / con cuernos que no deshonran" (3.25).

A general view of *El Caballero de Gracia* reveals a basically spiritual story grounded in Spain's religious history. The imagery is predominantly verbal, although allegorical and scenic elements occur sporadically.

DOÑA BEATRIZ DE SILVA

The life of Beatriz de Silva (1424-1490), founder of Toledo's Convent of the Conceptionists, was the inspiration for Tirso de Molina's historic-religious play *Doña Beatriz de Silva* (1619-1621).[3] Although the main emphasis is on Doña Beatriz's life, the royal courts of Portugal and Castile receive attention, thus introducing a worldly element into the predominantly religious story. In the first two acts, where the religious factor is subdued, Tirso included much historical material that contributes to the play's aesthetic value. The third act is predominately religious; however, the historical aspect is never abandoned.

In the opening scenes, Beatriz and her cousin Isabel prepare to leave Lisbon and journey to Castile, where Isabel will wed King John II. The marriage has been arranged by Don Alvaro de Luna of Castile and Don Alvaro de Girón of Portugal. Although the bride and groom have never met, each gladly accepts the arrangement. The issue is clouded when Don Alvaro de Girón, by mistake, shows the king a picture of Beatriz instead of Isabel. Instantly, the king falls in love with the likeness in this picture and when the two Portuguese girls are ushered into his presence, he declares his love to Beatriz. The mistaken identity is cleared quickly, to the satisfaction of all except Isabel. Even after the wedding, she cannot extinguish the flame of jealousy that tortures her. For this reason, she constantly tries to arrange a suitable marriage for her lady-in-waiting, thinking that once married, she will not pose a threat. In truth, and almost against his will, the king is attracted to Beatriz so much that he hesitates to sanction a marriage for her.

Isabel reaches a breaking point when she discovers that the king has written a note to Beatriz. In a fit of anger, the queen forces her cousin into a closet, where she plans to leave her until she dies. After three days of silent suffering, Beatriz is released through a miracle wrought by the Virgin. Mary explains that she is releasing Beatriz to propagate a movement dedicated to establishing the veracity of the Immaculate Conception. Spiritually reborn, Beatriz eschews her frivolous past and assumes the task before her. Isabel and King John assure Beatriz of her safety and pronounce their blessings on her holy cause.

A subplot in the play concerning Beatriz's brother, Juan de Meneses, mirrors the main plot. Juan is captivated by Leonor, even though her marriage to Frederick of Germany has already been planned. When he dares to confess his love after the wedding, the outraged queen slaps his

---

[3]Cotarelo y Mori, 2:xix.

face. Nursing his wounded honor, Juan reflects on the values of courtly life. He concludes that a religious life is the only one of true value; whereupon, he becomes a meditative hermit, assuming the name Fray Amador, "cortesano de Dios" (3.1).

The only religious image in the second act is inspired by Leonor's blow to Juan de Meneses. The incident takes place in Rome, a setting that leads Melgar to make a rather crude analogy, based on the double meaning of "Cardenal" (cardinal, welt), in which Juan's face is Rome, and the five fingerprints are cardinals clad in red.

> *Quiere en esta ocasión*
> *tu amor a Roma te iguales,*
> *que en prueba de esas señales*
> *fuera (porque te autorices)*
> *tu cara, a estar sin narices,*
> *Roma con sus Cardenales.*   (2.19)

Melgar continues with another pun on the words "fifth" and "sixth" in a veiled reference to Pope Sixtus and his successor, Pope Paul V.

> *Cinco en la cara te ha puesto;*
> *si fue favor no me espanto,*
> *mas favor que duele tanto*
> *más es quinto que no sexto.*   (2.19)

Many images are formed around the Virgin Mary and the Immaculate Conception. She is praised metaphorically in images of light that reflect her radiance as "Aurora pura," "Alba, Estrella, Luna, Sol" (3.1), and "sol del Cielo, luz de día" (3.8). Her purity is again extolled in terms of light when Beatriz, using images of the sun and clouds, explains the significance of the halo.

> *No hay en vos (mis ojos) nube;*
> *que por eso os cerca el sol,*
> *siendo sus rayos pestañas*
> *de su esfera guarnición.*   (3.1)

In the same scene, Beatriz interprets the blue and white of the Virgin's robe as elements of Heaven.

Images of Adam and Eve are invoked as Mary clarifies the interpretation of the virginal garments. By virtue of Adam's original sin, all humans are considered impure; however, Mary is the exception. Her robe is a physical testament of her purity: "cándido, limpio, sin nota, / sin pelo de imperfección" (3.2). Later, Beatriz will be instructed to adopt the same symbolic colors for her nuns: "lo blanco de su pureza, / lo azul del cielo a que aspiras" (3.9). Continuing the analogy to the original man and woman, Mary, by means of a catachresis, declares her purity as opposed to Eve's sinful nature.

> Si Eva fue mujer del suelo,
> la celeste mujer soy
> que estoy del cielo vestida.   (3.1)

Mary initiates the discussion of the Immaculate Conception when she describes the miracle of Jesus' birth in terms of clothing. God is the weaver, Jesus is the cloth, and Mary is the seamstress who will give form to the material.

> Yo soy la priviligiada
> cuya cándida creación
> hecha por dios ab initio
> para su Madre eligió;
> que habiéndose de vestir
> la tela que amor tejió,
> quiso preservar sin mancha
> en mí.   (3.1)

Saint Paul called Jesus the fruit of the Divine Conception, a second Adam. Mary adopts this metaphor as she contrasts the two Adams.

> si Pablo llamó
> a mi segundo hijo Adán
> siendo el primero en rigor,
> hombre de tierra terreno
> y hombre juntamente y Dios,
> celeste el Adán segundo.   (3.1)

The confusing line, "a mi segundo hijo Adán" is best interpreted as "a mi hijo segundo Adán." Mary refers to the first Adam as an earthly being ("hombre de tierra terrena") and to Christ, by virtue of his being both earthly and heavenly ("hombre y Dios"), as a celestial Adam—God in human image.

Religious images centered around Beatriz de Silva are introduced in the final act only, after her conversion. The Virgin Mary's initial meeting with Beatriz accents the superficial values held by the beautiful lady-in-waiting. Mary compares Beatriz to the faithful nuns of the Church in an antithetical image.

> *Las damas de mi Palacio,*
> *Beatriz, siguen el olor*
> *de mi pureza virgínea*
> *Y Angélica incorrupción;*
> *no, como tú, el tiempo pierden,*
> *que tanto el cuerdo estimó*
> *en galas y vanidades,*
> *incendios del torpe amor.* (3.1)

A contrite Beatriz immediately vows to emulate the nuns' constancy: "Su esclava, mi Niña, soy" (3.1).

Mary approaches Beatriz on familiar ground when she suggests that the young girl become a nun. The language of the court alludes to a spiritual hierarchy:

> *Si soy Reina, como afirmas*
> *¿Ser mi dama no es mejor*
> *que la de la Reina Isabel?* (3.1)

After Beatriz completely dedicates herself to the Christian cause, Saint Anthony makes an analogy between Beatriz and the Virgin. Each is a virgin and each will be a mother (Mary will be the Mother of Christ, and Beatriz will be mother in the convent).

> *Virgin has de ser, y madre,*
> *que así, de algún modo, imitas*
> *a quien siendo Madre y Virgin*
> *a Dios que se humane obliga.* (3.9)

An additional analogy is suggested in Beatriz's farewell letter to the king. She tells about her miraculous salvation from death in words that hint of Christ's return from the dead: "que resucité al tercer día" (3.6).

The major scenic images of the third act, which are as elaborate as those found in Tirso's hagiographic plays, are designed around the appearances of the Virgin and Saint Anthony. At first, Mary's presence is indicated only by the sound of her voice, but she soon appears high above the stage, standing on a cloud and wearing long robes and a crown. The traditional presentation of the Virgin of the Immaculate Conception is completed with a halo of light illuminating her head (3.1). As she converses with Beatriz, Mary mentions Juan de Meneses, whereupon a rear alcove is unveiled, revealing Don Juan. Dressed like a hermit, he appears with Saint Jeronimo, who holds up his hand to guide him over a rocky mountain. Hanging on a nearby tree are Juan's armor and plumed hat—symbols of his courtly life. Visually, the scene portrays one of God's angels offering support to a man who has abandoned the vanities of the court. This alcove is quickly covered, and Mary continues her discourse.

At the conclusion of the conversation, Beatriz, who has been released from the closet, returns to her cell in a physical act that reveals her spiritual confidence in the Virgin. In the next scene (3.2), her faith is proven correct as she emerges from the closet before an astonished king and queen.

Like the Virgin Mary, Saint Anthony speaks from offstage before making his entry (3.7). Celestial music announces his arrival as he appears on a platform above the stage. As he addresses Beatriz, he turns to theological subjects, while vignettes appear to emphasize the import of his words. He mentions Pope Sixtus IV and Pope Paul V, the citizens of Toledo and Seville, and, finally, Don Juan de Meneses is recalled. In the order listed, each person or group is presented, until the stage and area surrounding it are crowded with people who have worked to affirm the Immaculate Conception. The scene is begun and concluded with appropriate music, thus increasing the effect of an elaborate religious pageant.

The purpose of Saint Anthony's elaborate presentation is to bolster Beatriz's confidence in her cause. When Isabel and John join the pageant and add their blessings, Beatriz joyfully continues her journey to Toledo, where she will establish the worthy Convent of the Conceptionists.

LA ROMERA DE SANTIAGO

Tirso's travels in Galicia provided inspiration for *La romera de Santiago* (1619 or 1620), a play that eulogizes the sacred shrine of Spain's patron saint while presenting a traditional plot of love entanglements within a religious atmosphere. The opening scenes present Ordoño, king of Leon, as he commends his noblest count, Lisuardo, for his victories over the Moors. As a reward for his exceptional services, Ordoño has arranged for his sister, Linda, to marry Lisuardo. The bethrothed couple is ecstatic, but before the marriage can be consummated, Lisuardo must journey to England to contract a marriage for Ordoño with Marguerite, daughter of King Henry.

Soon after Lisuardo leaves, he encounters a beautiful, young penitent returning to Castile after visiting the shrine at Santiago. She identifies herself as Sol, Countess of Lara, daughter of the illustrious Don Manrique. Lisuardo instantly falls in love with her and instructs his soldiers to seize her. In the brief scuffle that ensues, Sol is wounded and her honor tarnished, after which Lisuardo abandons her. Dishonored and enraged, Sol presents her complaints to King Ordoño, who immediately promises to avenge her. Garci-Fernández, Sol's cousin and Linda's most ardent suitor, also vows to seek vengeance for his kinswoman.

Lisuardo returns, is jailed, and sentenced to the gallows, but with Linda's aid, he escapes. This done, Garci-Fernández demands that Ordoño take the place of his vassal in a duel; Sol follows suit by challenging Linda. As the contest begins, Lisuardo returns to redeem his king and accept full responsibility for his actions. Garci-Fernández relents when he sees this noble side of Lisuardo and offers him Sol as his bride. This accomplished, Linda is free to marry Garci-Fernández, while Ordoño, in a burst of magnanimity, frees the servants from jail, amidst an atmosphere of merriment.

Throughout the play, the influence of Santiago prevails, giving a religious undertone to the predominantly profane story. On traveling through Galicia, Lisuardo contemplates the vernal glories of nature that surround him. He interprets its beauty as an expression of God's voice and a reflection of Heaven.

> los arroyos pasamanos,
> bendiciendo con las lenguas
> que primero murmuraron
> al zafiro de los cielos
> la esmeralda de los prados,
> que a no gozallos tan triste
> de ausente y enamorado,
> fuera pasar por el cielo.   (1.13)

In a hyperbolic eulogy to Galicia, Lisuardo adds that no other place can offer as much spiritual aid as this land. Pilgrims, shipwreck victims, and captive Christians meet at the ancient sanctuary (1.13). The road that leads to the shrine is likened to the Milky Way when one of Lisuardo's soldiers reports that the heavenly constellation is referred to colloquially as the Santiago Way (1.13). In the same scene, Lisuardo's servant, Ramiro, in a bold comparison, observes that no other road is frequented as much as the path to Santiago—not even the road between Rome and Jerusalem.

The title character, Sol, is considered to be of Tirso's best feminine characters. Noble, chaste, fervently Catholic, she is the prototype of the Spanish noblewoman of her time.[4] The fact that Sol is a model Christian makes Lisuardo's attack on her even more detestable and accents the spiritual contrast between the two principal characters. A variety of religious images are employed to characterize her. Sol's beauty and spiritual radiance, suggested by her name, are affirmed in Lisuardo's metaphorical appraisal of her virtue: "tan peregrina milagro / de honestad y belleza" (1.14). The gracioso, Relox, concurs that her spiritual dedication is intense and contrasts sharply with the evil of Pontius Pilate. He calls her "querubín soberano" and then hyperbolically avows Sol's spiritual power: "que puede con los ojos / matar a Poncio Pilato" (1.15).

An image of Sol's humility is evinced in her penitent's dress and her determination to walk to and from the shrine (2.8). Another facet of her humility is revealed when, in a stream of metaphors, she curses her beauty as an obstacle in her search for spiritual purity.

> *este monstruo, esta escorpión*
> *a quien llaman hermosura*
> *(veneno fuera mejor),*
> *este basilisco humano,*
> *esta esfinje que nació*
> *para vender a su dueño*
> *de un parto con la traición.*   (2.8)

She continues this scourge with additional metaphors designed to illustrate her naturally modest character.

---

[4]Blanca de los Ríos, 2:1231.

Lisuardo's attack on the pious pilgrim coincides with an eclipse of the sun (2.8), an event that is interpreted as a symbol of God's displeasure. Sol's prayers for vengeance, "quejas al Cielo" (2.8), are delivered in a fervent but self-effacing manner. She seeks retribution with the ferocity of a wild beast, yet she feels that one as dishonored as she is dare not approach God ("el sol"): "no es justo que mire al sol" (2.8).

The Leonese king, Ordoño, is portrayed in several images as the traditional monarch who is a dispenser of justice, directly guided by God. Ordoño himself says that he is divinely inspired; hence, he cannot falter in his judgments.

> *Mas todo lo facilita*
> *la Justicia y la prudencia,*
> *porque el Rey que a Dios imita*
> *con humana providencia*
> *lo que importa solicita.*   (2.8)

When Sol seeks vengeance, Garci-Fernández reminds Ordoño that he is God's representative of earthly justice: "La Justicia, que en lugar / de Dios resplancece en ti" (2.8). He repeats this metaphorical thought in capsule form in the last act: "Sois de la Justicia espejo" (3.11). Linda also comments on the strict, but just, decisions made by her brother. When Lisuardo begs for clemency, Linda replies, in a paradoxical manner, that God's earthly representative cannot help him, but perhaps God will.

> *El rey ha de hacer de justicia,*
> *que son sus obligaciones;*
> *remédiete el Cielo.*   (3.6)

The underlying message contained in Linda's words is that when all earthly recourses fail, God is still available. Relox voices a similar philosophy, claiming he still has hope that God will release him from the prison tower, in spite of past deeds. When he says "puede alcanzar con Dios / un delincuente lacayo" (3.14), his words can be interpreted on a much broader spiritual level.

References to Moorish-Christian wars contribute to the historical aspect of *La romera de Santiago*. The opening scene contains a eulogy to Lisuardo's military prowess against the infidels, which, in part, relies on the use of metonymy.

tanta africana luna
metistes de esta ocasión
arrastrando por León.   (1.1)

When Lisuardo returns from England, Ordoño's soldiers immediately disarm him, causing the bewildered count to question the king's action in view of his past victories in religious wars. He also makes recourse to metonymies as he voices his complaint:.

¿A un hombre que sobre
la luna y sol ha puesto
con tantos hechos su nombre
y el de su Rey, manda el Rey
dar la espada, cuyo corte
tanto católico acero
y africano reconoce?   (3.11)

On two occasions, Tirso used costuming to create effective religious images. When Doña Sol and her servant appear onstage, they are clad in the coarse robes of penitents (1.14)—an external representation of spiritual humility. On seeing them, Lisuardo exclaims, "Del mismo cielo parece / que las habéis bajado," thereby giving vocal testimony of the image of their angelic spirits. Later, Lisuardo assumes the dress of a prisoner as he languishes in the prison tower, bound by heavy chains. On a spiritual plane, the chains may be viewed as evidence of his alienation from God. This idea is suggested when Lisuardo moans, "¿Qué infierno es éste?" (3.12).

Religious images are brought into the play sparingly in *La romera de Santiago*; however, references to the Shrine of Santiago, to the Christian-Moorish wars, and to the pious character of Lisuardo's victim combine to create a religious background for the profane story.

LAS QUINAS DE PORTUGAL

The admiration that Tirso de Molina felt for Portugal is clearly evident in *Las quinas de Portugal* (1638), one of the playwright's last known dramatic works. Seeking inspiration in that country's august history, the play deals with the origins of its monarchy and the life and deeds of Don Alfonso Enríquez, count and first king of Portugal.[5]

In Tirso's dramatized account, Alfonso meets the hermit Giraldo, who convinces the king to rededicate his efforts to eradicate the Moorish kingdoms on Portuguese soil. Since the most powerful Moorish king in that area, Ismael, is headquartered in Santarén, he becomes Alfonso's immediate target. Before the battle, the count retires to his quarters to consult the Bible and pray for guidance. His efforts are rewarded by a vision of Christ, who assures him that his forces will be victorious in spite of the overwhelming odds in favor of the Moors. As a token of divine support, Christ hands Alfonso a banner with the arms of Portugal emblazoned on it, promising that soon it will wave over the Moorish towers. The soldiers, inspired by Alfonso's heavenly zeal, face the enemy with redoubled courage. Ismael is killed, the banner is raised over Santarén, and Alfonso is proclaimed Portugal's first king. In the last scene, the new monarch urges his countrymen to accompany him to church where they will offer thanksgiving to God.

In traditional *comedia* style, a secondary plot intertwines with the main story. Ismael falls in love with Leonor, a beautiful Portuguese girl. Her capture and subsequent escape from Ismael's quarters present an opportunity to contrast the two religions and cultures. True to his calling, the Mercedarian dramatist highlights the virtues of Christianity and blasphemes Mohammedanism.

Laudatory images inspired by Alfonso are numerous. In spite of his worldly power, the monarch sees himself as God's subservient. His self-description begins with a negative metaphor and concludes with two positive ones.

> *No soy rey, yo, ni blasón*
> *tan arrogante procuro,*
> *Conde sí, defensa y muro*
> *de Portugal, Dios su dueño.*   (3.2)

In his dual role as soldier and religious man, Alfonso is compared to similar biblical characters: first to David, then to Martha and Mary (2.1), and finally to Moses and his successor, Joshua: "Moisés en la oración /

---

[5]Blanca de los Ríos, 3:1319.

y Josué con la espada" (2.2). Sensing the spiritual bond that exists between Man and God, Alfonso describes the condition with the aphoristic statement, "Yo en vos y vos conmigo" (3.4). Further proof of the count's loyalty to and understanding of God is evidenced when he refuses to raise his eyes to meet those of Christ.

> *no necesito*
> *veros con ojos corpóreos*
> *mientras en la tierra vivo.*   (3.5)

Images of war and warriors take on a religious character on several occasions. Giraldo alludes to the Christian's lance and the cause for which it stands in three metonymies ("hierro," "sangre," and "agua"): "hierro que abrió de amor todo el abismo, / sangre a la redención, agua al bautismo" (1.3). The hermit continues with metonymies to refer to past religious conquests.

> *Con católicas mitras las cabezas*
> *ciñó de Braga, hispana primacía,*
> *de Oporto y de Coimbra.*   (1.3)

Santarén was once claimed for the Christians by Alfonso's father, Enrique. As the son plans his reconquest, he uses the words "cruz" and "luna" to indicate the two conflicting religions.

> *tremolando en sus almenas*
> *la cruz que a Jerusalén*
> *restauró mi padre Enrique,*
> *sus lunas postre a los pies.*   (1.10)

All Christians rally for the Moorish attack, causing Alfonso to comment, "cada cual es un espejo / de la fe que defendemos" (3.1). The city's return to the Christians is metaphorically proclaimed: "Ya es Santarén cristiana; / ya Sión, si fue Babel" (1.22).

Religious imagery is most elaborate in references to Christ and God. In a soliloquy, Alfonso praises Christ in a series of metaphors.

> *¡Oh nombre siempre inefable!*
> *¡oh grano eterno de trigo*
> *que en Belén, casa de pan,*
> *de la espiga virgen quiso*
> *nacer!*   (3.4)

He continues, utilizing the image of bread, while alluding to Old Testament events.

> Pan que maná en el desierto
> tierno, sabroso y melifluo,
> fortaleció cuarenta años
> el pueblo fiel contra Egipto.
> . . . .
> pan panal, que, león primero,
> cordero ya puro y limpio
> de la boca formidable
> para Sanson colmena hizo,
> pan que asegura victorias
> a Abraham contra los cinco
> reyes infieles, que a Lot
> osaron llevar captivo.   (3.4)

When Christ appears before Alonso, the overwhelmed count gives voice to a series of paraphrastic allusions to the Son of God.

> ¡Oh Juez, ya todo clemencia!
> . . . .
> ¡Oh pan que levanta el bieldo
> de la cruz en fe que limpio
> dice la vil sinagoga!
> ¡miramus in panem lignum!
> ¡Oh fruta de promisión!   (3.5)

Two images are centered around Christ's wounds. Before the battle, Christ tells Alfonso that His wound will serve as five shields (3.5). Having attained the victory, Alfonso alludes to Christ's wounds as payment for Man's salvation, after which he contrasts his own baseness with Christ's purity by means of a chiasmus: "llagas por mi bien abiertas / aunque las abrió mi mal" (3.14).

Continuing in this vein, he describes Christ's redemptive mission on earth, alluding to the Cross as the receptacle of Christ's body.

> árbol del segundo Adán,
> que la fruta del primero
> venenosa, remediáis

> *con ese enjerto pendiente,*
> *Dios eterno, hombre mortal.*   (3.14)

The lines are multi-metaphorical. "Arbol" refers to the Cross, Christ is the "segundo Adán," "fruta" represents Adam's original sin, and the last line is a commentary on the duality of Jesus' nature. The contrast of the two Adams lends an antithetical tone to the entire image.

Tirso introduces scenic devices on several occasions to underline his religious message. To indicate the holiness of the impending battle, Gonzalo enters with a large silver shield emblazoned with a blue cross. The soldier comments on its symbolism in alliterative fashion:

> *cruz azul, señal del celo*
> *con que restituyó al cielo*
> *de Dios el sepulcro santo.*   (1.6)

Following this explanation, the soldiers kneel before the shield, placing their hands on the Cross to demonstrate their dedication to the Christian cause (1.6).

In the third act, Alfonso appears onstage alone, holding the open Bible (3.2). The simplicity of the scene serves to accent the pure faith of a Christian king who seeks divine guidance in his earthly activities.

After the battle, a throne bearing the crucified Christ is lowered from above stage. This image represents God's approval of Alfonso's attack on the infidels. Angels are also lowered, while a chorus enters singing the *Christus regnat*. To confirm His presence, Christ releases one hand from the Cross and presents Portugal's banner to Alfonso, directing him to place it over Santarén (3.5). The entire display resembles a religious tableau.

The last scene in the play contains two visual displays of religious import. To symbolize the Christian victory, Alfonso places the Portuguese banner over Santarén's walls. As the Cross is raised to the accompanying sounds of flageolets, the entire company falls to its knees, emphasizing the reverence of the occasion. In the background, a pile of slain Moors gives visual commentary to the bloodiness of the religious wars and indicates the fall of Mohammedanism. With this vivid portrayal of Christian triumph, the play concludes.

CHAPTER V

THE PHILOSOPHIC-RELIGIOUS MASTERPIECES

Two philosophic, religious dramas that consider the theological problems of spiritual salvation, *El condenado por desconfiado* (1614-1615) and *El burlador de Sevilla* (c.1620), are Tirso de Molina's best-known plays. Each is dominated by two basic concepts: free will, by which Man can save himself through a positive desire to seek forgiveness, and the responsibility of persons to account to God for their actions. It is in the approach to these concepts that the plays differ.

In the more complex play, *El condenado por desconfiado*, Enrico is forgiven a life of crime through sincere faith and repentance, while Paulo, the hermit, is condemned because he believed in predestination so strongly that it inhibited the exercising of his free will. Don Juan, Tirso's famous libertine of *El burlador de Sevilla*, did not lack faith in God; however, he refused to look beyond the present and place his actions in the proper perspective in relation to his spiritual life. Believing that there was always time to repent at some nebulous future time, he wasted his life until it was too late to seek forgiveness.

When the priest-poet dramatized his theological doctrines, he employed a variety of poetic images to depict the spiritual state of Man. A study of the two plays reveals the skill with which Tirso united art and religion.

EL CONDENADO POR DESCONFIADO

During the first half of the seventeenth century, a bitter theological debate raged in Spain between the Dominicans and the Jesuits. The conflict began in 1558 with the publication of *Liberi arbitrii cum gratiae donis, . . . concordia*, by the Jesuit Luis de Molina. In the *Concordia*, which addressed the problem of reconciling the apparent conflict between human will and the efficacy of God's grace, the Jesuit proposed that whereas grace prompts the will, it does not propel persons to any direct course of action; moreover, the free consent of the will is a basic requirement for obtaining efficacious grace.[1] According to this theory, the doctrine of predestination is disavowed. Molina also held that a distinction between sufficient and efficacious grace was not necessary, claiming that sufficient grace becomes efficacious when the individual wills it.[2] This theological interpretation, designated as Molinism, was soundly refuted by the Dominicans and several other religious groups in Spain who claimed that such conclusions were presumptuous on the part of humans, since they could not comprehend the complexities of the Divine Spirit.[3] It was this theological conflict that prompted Tirso de Molina to write *El condenado por desconfiado*, a dramatized consideration of the problem of free will, grace, and predestination.

The tone of the entire play is allegorical, with the contemplative Paulo and the active Enrico representing two types of men who carve their destinies in distinct fashions. The path of their lives and their ultimate ends are a vivid affirmation of Padre Molina's doctrine. Paulo, who has spent ten years as an exemplary hermit in the hills outside Naples, dares to question God about his ultimate fate: "¿he de ir a vuestro Cielo o al infierno?" (1.3). Disguised as an angel, the devil tells Paulo that his fate will be the same as that of Enrico of Naples. Paulo imme-

---

[1]*A Catholic Dictionary*, ed. Donald Attwater, 3rd ed. (New York: MacMillan, 1958) 328.

[2]*Encyclopedia of Philosophy*, ed. Paul Edwards (New York: MacMillan and the Free Press) 7:338.

[3]Vossler, 77.

diately journeys to Naples, where he is horrified to discover that Enrico
is a living example of man's depravity. With his hopes of attaining
Heaven shattered, since he assumes that Enrico will be condemned to
Hell, Paulo throws off his penitent's robe and plunges into a life of
crime.

A closer look at the young Enrico reveals that he is not totally de-
praved. He is redeemed by two features: a sincere love and respect for
his father and a firm belief in God. When he is ultimately sentenced to
death, he refuses to offend God with a confession; whereupon, his father,
Anareto, insists that there is no other way. Minutes before his death, Enrico confesses, thus obtaining entry into Heaven and pardon for his past
sins. Abruptly, Paulo awakens to the fact that he has been deceived by
the devil; however, his crimes are of such magnitude now that he dares
not ask God's pardon. With his will thus preventing an approach to God,
Paulo dies bereft of divine grace and is condemned to suffer the eternal
flames of Hell.

The concluding lines of the play condemn humanity's audacity to
prejudge God's capacity to forgive. As Paulo says,

> *fui desconfiado*
> *de la gran piedad de Dios,*
> . . . .
> *¡Malditos mis padres sean*
> *mil veces, pues me engendraron!*
> *Y yo también sea maldito,*
> *pues que fui desconfiado.*   (3.22)

The simplicity of his words, pregnant with anguish, expressive of the
desolation of his condition, contrast sharply with those of Enrico, "En
Dios confío" (3.15). By contrasting the religious opinion taken by each
man, Tirso leads his audience to conclude that efficacious grace is free
to all who seek it.

Poetic figures describing the two main characters succeed in accent-
ing the opposing religious attitudes. The moment Paulo asks to know his
fate, the devil refers to him as "el desconfiado de Dios y de su poder"
(1.6), although Paulo does not yet recognize his fatal flaw. Upon arriving
in Naples, he asks his servant Pedrisco to walk on him, as an external
display of his spiritual humility (1.11). When the second act begins,
however, Paulo has seen the infamous Enrico and abandons all effort to

be godly. Pedrisco comments on the metamorphosis in an antithetical image.

> *verte ayer, señor,*
> *ayunar con tal fervor,*
> *y en la oración ocupado,*
> *en tu Dios arrebatado,*
> . . . .
> *y en esta selva escondida*
> *verte hoy con tanta violencia,*
> *capitán de forajida*
> *gente.* (2.9)

Notwithstanding his firm resolve to imitate Enrico's life, Paulo is filled with desperation as he labors under the false assumption that he is a condemned soul. In an emotional hyperbole, he claims that the flood of tears in which his soul is drowning is surpassed only by the waters that flow into a river (2.17). When his new life is firmly established, Paulo asserts, "Soy Enrico en las crueldades" (3.20) to give metaphorical measure to his deeds.

Several images are centered around Paulo's fall from godliness. The devil is the first to gleefully observe his double weaknesses of doubt and pride; hence, when the devil speaks of these two qualities he is alluding to an eminent fall.

> *Este, aunque ha side tan santo,*
> *duda de la fe, pues vemos*
> *que quiere del mismo Dios,*
> *estando en duda, saberlo.*
> *En la soberbia también*
> *ha pecado: caso es cierto.*
> *Nadie como yo lo sabe,*
> *pues por soberbio padezco.* (1.4)

Lack of faith is the single cause for Paulo's fall—a condition that is clearly indicated as the doubting hermit listens to Enrico recount the events of his sinful life. Paulo jumps to the false conclusion that such a life is unconditionally condemned—and his as well, since he believes the false angel's prediction that their fates will be similar. The following lines, which allude to eternal punishment, are a pathetic demonstration of Paulo's lack of faith.

> *Ya me parece que siento*
> *que aquellas voraces llamas*
> *van abrazando mi cuerpo.*   (1.13)

Although Paulo tries to justify his deviation from the pure life, the moment he enters into crime, his fall is definitive. His words, in antithetical form, allude to his spiritual ruin.

> *Pues si es ansí, tener quiero*
> *en el mundo buena vida*
> *pues tan triste fin espero.*
> *Los pasos pienso seguir*
> *de Enrico.*   (1.13)

The same sentiments are paraphrased later, still in antithetical form, but made more vivid by the use of catachresis.

> *Mi adverso fin no resisto,*
> *pues mi desaventura he visto,*
> *y da claro testimonio*
> *el vestirme de demonio*
> *y el desnudarme de Cristo.*   (2.17)

In an extended metaphor, the bandit Paulo comments on his sins in terms of a tree. He promises to complement each branch of the tree with the head of a victim. Like the tree, his fruits will be abundant.

> *he de dar a cada rama*
> *cada día una cabeza,*
> *Vosotros dais, por ser graves,*
> *frutos al hombre suaves;*
> *mas yo con tales racimos*
> *pienso dar frutos opimos*
> *a las voladoras aves.*   (2.9)

Images devoted to the metaphorical characterization of Enrico are equally profuse. He is condemned as "el diablo" (1.9), "ese hombre / que en vida está ya ardiendo en los infiernos" (3.21), and one of the "rufianes de Belcebú" (1.10). In one scene, Enrico urges his cohorts to recount their past crimes, promising to present the winner a crown of laurels (1.12). The act is a reverse version of human accountability to God, with Enrico assuming the identity of Satan as he rewards evil.

Later, a contrite Enrico confesses his sins to God, describing himself in derogatory hyperboles.

> Yo he side el hombre más malo
> que la luz llegó a alcanzar
> deste mundo, el que ha hecho
> más que arenas tiene el mar
> ofensas.   (3.15)

In spite of his overtly sinful life, Enrico never abandons his faith in God's extreme mercy: "mas siempre tengo esperanza / en que tengo de salvarme" (2.17). The dramatic difference between Paulo and Enrico lies in their position toward God's grace. When Paulo says, "Muy desconfiado soy," Enrico replies, "Aquesta desconfianza te tiene de condenar" (2.17).

Images of God and His mercy are introduced to reinforce the theological nature of the play. He is addressed on various occasions with the following epithets: "el Justicia mayor del Cielo" (1.3), "el Juez más supremo y recto" (1.4), "Juez piadoso, sabio, recto" (1.13), and "mar de misericordia" (3.15). Pedrisco claims of God that "vuestro inmenso amor / todo lo imposible doma" (1.1), while Enrico begins his prayer with a traditional salutation:

> Señor piadoso y eterno,
> que en vuestro alcazar pisáis
> cándidos montes de estrellas,
> mi petición escuchad.   (3.15)

Since God's clemency ("misericordia") is the axis around which the play turns, it is emphasized often with poetic images. Of prime importance is the fact that God endowed each individual with the gift of free will, making him responsible for the acceptance or rejection of divine grace. Man's complex nature is described in the following image:

> aquella imperfección
> diole Dios libre albedrío,
> y fragilidad le dio
> al cuerpo y al alma; luego

dio potestad con acción
de pedir misericordia.   (2.11)

The shepherd defines grace or divine mercy in hyperbolic terms in response to Paulo's question.

Aunque sus ofensas sean
más que átomos hay del sol,
y que estrellas tiene el cielo,
y rayos la luna dio,
y peces el mar salado
en sus concavos guardo.
Esta es su misericordia.   (2.11)

Enrico is also aware of God's compassion, as seen in Enrico's paraphrase of salvation.

puesto que no va fundada
mi esperanza en obras mías,
sino en saber que se humana
Dios con el más pecador,
y con su piedad se salva.   (2.17)

In like manner, the venerable Anareto instructs his son to seek God's mercy, so that his impending death will be transformed to eternal life in Heaven. The idea is expressed in a paradox: "siendo perdonados, / será vida lo que es muerte" (3.15).

Speaking of God's mercy, the shepherd tells Paulo that the Crucifixion is a representation of God's ultimate sacrifice for humanity. In the following lines, the sufferings of the Cross are expressed in metaphors, while the last six lines refer to the Virgin Birth and describe Christ in crystalline images.

aquella sangre
que liberal derramó,
haciendo un mar a su cuerpo,
que amoroso dividió
en cinco sangrientos ríos;
que su espíritu formó
nueve meses en el vientre,
de aquella que mereció

ser Virgin cuando fue Madre,
y claro oriente del sol,
que como clara vidriera,
sin que la rompiese, entró.   (2.11)

On a broad scope, *El condenado por desconfiado* is an allegory; how-ever, in certain sections of the drama, the allegorical is more apparent, such as in Enrico's relationship with his father. Anareto assumes the po-sition of a heavenly father in the eyes of his son, who reveres him as a superior being. Enrico conceals his sinful life from his father, and while in his presence, Enrico can do no evil (2.5). Similarly, sinners try to con-ceal their sins from God and are not motivated to yield to sin while in His presence. When Enrico escapes by sea, he laments that his father cannot accompany him: "aunque en el alma bien sé yo que os llevo" (2.8). The idea, on a spiritual level, is that God is carried in the heart even though His physical presence is denied. In the last act, Anareto visits his son in jail, where he insists that he either confess to God or be disowned as his son (3.10). His act is symbolic of God's rejection of all who refuse to con-fess their sins and ask for pardon.

One of the major allegories of the play revolves around the little shep-herd who is seeking his lost sheep. He is easily identified as a Christ fig-ure seeking lost souls. When he first appears, he is weaving a crown of flowers that he intends to offer to the wayward sheep as soon as it returns to the fold (2.11). The crown is a symbol of heavenly reward awaiting all who seek God. The allegory is continued in the next act when the shep-herd returns; this time he is destroying the garland he had previously woven, because the sheep will not return (3.17). When he says, "engañ-ada y necia / dejó a quien la amaba," the symbolism of Paulo's refusal to return to God is obvious. The allegorical nature of the scene is openly averred after the shepherd leaves and when Paulo observes, "La historia parece / de mi vida aquesta" (3.18).

Paulo's painful death is a scenic allegory portraying the destiny of one who abandons God. After death, Paulo appears engulfed in flames, recognizing too late the price he must pay for his lack of confidence. He sinks into a pit and flames leap onto the stage in a dramatic representa-tion of his descent to Hell (3.22).

Throughout the play, scenic devices are used to present religious im-ages. In the first act, the devil appears in corporal form, seated on a rock, yet hidden from Paulo's view. Only when he assumes the identity of an angel does he reveal himself to Paulo (1.4). An external display of Paulo's depravity is his appearance in bandit's garb (2.4), a costume that contrasts with his former hermit's robes (1.1). Paulo appears as a hermit again in the second act when he tries to convince Enrico to confess so that he may discover the extent of his sinfulness. In this scene, Paulo's clothes are a direct contrast to his spiritual state—a fact that is admitted when he casts off the hypocritical robes. As he removes them, he likens his actions to that of a snake shedding its skin. The evil connotation of the snake cannot be overlooked as he says, "En mis torpezas resbalo / y a la culebra me igualo" (2.16).

In the last act, Enrico is alone in his cell, pondering his fate. Not only is he denied physical freedom, but his unconfessed acts are also shackles that prevent him from attaining spiritual freedom. While he is in this confinement, Enrico hears a voice calling him. At his insistence, the voice assumes a shadowy form and provides an escape door in the cell. As the prisoner contemplates flight, another voice offstage sings that if Enrico hopes to live he must remain (3.5). Much later, the enlightened Enrico identifies the opposing sources of the voices.

> La enigma he entendido ya
> de la voz y de la sombra:
> la voz era angelical,
> y la sombra era el demonio.   (2.15)

The spiritual climax of the play, Enrico's salvation, is briefly but elaborately represented onstage. While celestial music plays, a rear alcove is unveiled, revealing two angels who are carrying Enrico's soul to Heaven. As soon as Paulo comments briefly that "dos ángeles llevan una alma gloriosa / a la excelsa esfera" (3.18), the alcove is covered, leaving the sinner to consider the implication of the display. In this presentation, Tirso clearly indicated his agreement with the Molinists' theory that through faith and exercise of free will, God's saving grace is attainable.

EL BURLADOR DE SEVILLA

Tirso de Molina's most famous dramatic work is *El burlador de Sevilla*, a theatrical treatise on the theological problem of free will. The unique character of the protagonist, Don Juan Tenorio, has provided inspiration for more than three and a half centuries to poets, dramatists, and authors the world over.

The simply constructed plot traces the amorous escapades of Don Juan Tenorio, a Spanish nobleman whose erotic nature leads him to seduce every woman with whom he comes in contact. In spite of the moralizing admonitions of his servant Catalinón, Don Juan operates on the belief that God's mercy is so great and long-suffering that forgiveness will be granted whenever it is asked. This philosophy, expressed in the oft-repeated line, "Tan largo me lo fiáis," leads the dissolute youth to commit a series of seductions that he lightly justifies in his own eyes. While in Naples, he enters the bedroom of Isabel, bride-to-be of his best friend, Octavio. Thinking it is her intended husband, Isabel recognizes too late she has been duped by the infamous trickster.

On the way to Seville, Don Juan seduces a young fisherwoman, Tisbea, and Aminta, a beautiful shepherdess. Arriving in Seville, he immediately enters into new amorous activities. In a cruel joke, Don Juan disguises himself as his friend, the Marquis de Mota, to gain entry to Doña Ana's bedroom. When Ana discovers the deception she cries out, causing her father, Gonzalo de Ulloa, to attack the imposter. In the ensuing scuffle, Gonzalo is killed, while the trickster escapes by way of the balcony.

Don Juan joyfully continues his libertine ways until the night he chances upon Gonzalo's tomb. In a youthful display of bravado, Don Juan approaches the statue of his victim, tweaks his beard, and invites him to supper the next night. Gonzalo surprises his host, not only by appearing at the appointed time, but by insisting that he reciprocate the invitation the following night. Since his fear of being deemed a coward is greater than that of attending the cemetery festivity, Don Juan is driven to accept the statue's invitation. When he appears in the cemetery, Don Juan is suddenly confronted by death and the fires of Hell. Having procrastinated too long in seeking God's forgiveness, he is swept to eternal punishment.

The poetry employed by Tirso in his theological observations is steeped in Renaissance inspiration, especially in the references to Don Juan's nocturnal adventures; however, the voice of the Christian moralist becomes equally prominent in the last act. The general movement in the play is a gradual shift from the profane to the religious, but if the profane elements are interpreted as negatives in one's attempt to gain salvation, they can also be considered part of the general religious framework.

Don Juan is the inspiration for a variety of negative images of theological import. His uncle Pedro avers that "pienso que el demonio / en él tomó forma humana" (1.9). Batricio, the unfortunate shepherd who loses his bride to Don Juan, agrees, observing, "Imagino / que el demonio le envió" (2.21). Overcome with shame when he hears of his son's dishonorable conduct, Diego cries out, "¡Qué mal me pagas / el amor que te he tenido" (3.17). On a theological level, his words can be interpreted as the Heavenly Father's admonishing a sinner for his ingratitude.

The sins of Don Juan are of double concern to his father, for he fears not only his son's ultimate punishment, but also his own, should God seek vengeance through the father. For these reasons, Diego pledges to make restitution for his son's misdeeds. In view of this he prays, "rayos contra mí no baje / si es mi hijo tan malo" (3.25). Throughout the play, Don Juan's escapades are living examples of his moral decay, as can be seen in the seductions of Isabela (1.1), Tisbea (1.16), and Aminta (3.8), in the betrayal of his friend, the Marquis de Mota (2.13), and in the murder of Gonzalo (2.14).

The belief that persons must ultimately be accountable for their actions is a recurrent theme in the play. This theme is particularly voiced by Catalinón. Many critics have said that Catalinón represents Don Juan's conscience; however, considering the protagonist's complete lack of moral awareness, perhaps it is more logical to interpret the gracioso's moralizing voice as that of the Church. In the following conversational exchanges, Catalinón alludes to God's vengeance while Don Juan repeatedly rejects the idea.

Catalinón.   *Los que fingís y engañáis*
              las mujeres desa suerte
              lo pagaréis en la muerte.
Don Juan.   *¡Qué largo me lo fiáis!*   (1.15)
Catalinón.   *No lo apruebo.*
              Tu pretendes que escapemos
              una vez, señor, burlados,
              que el que vive de burlar
              burlado habrá de escapar

Don Juan.
>
> *de una vez.*
> *¿Predicador*
> *te vuelves, impertinente?*   (2.9)

Later, the servant cautions his master to consider the consequences should he persist in the seduction of Aminta. His words suggest the vengeful God of the Old Testament: "suele Dios tomar venganza" (3.6). Catilinón continues moralizing in a poetic antithesis that alludes to eternal punishment for an ill-spent life. Don Juan's ready excuse is to be expected.

Catalinón.
> *Mira lo que has hecho, y mira*
> *que hasta la muerte, señor,*
> *es corta la mayor vida;*
> *que hay tras la muerte infierno.*

Don Juan.
> *Si tan largo me lo fiáis,*
> *vengan engaños.*   (3.6)

In a metaphorical allusion to God, Diego also warns his son that vengeance is nigh ("es Juez fuerte / Dios en la muerte"), in spite of Don Juan's mistaken idea that death is far in the future: "De aquí allá hay gran jornada" (2.11).

On one occasion, Tisbea also puts on a moralizing hat when she cautions her lover in an aphoristic manner: "que hay Dios y hay muerte." The libertine's predictable reply, "¡Qué largo me lo fiáis!" (1.16), is twice repeated in the conversation as he brushes off moral obligations.

Tirso's metaphysical considerations of death and eternity are visually presented in the last half of the third act when Don Juan reads the inscription of Gonzalo's tomb and notes that the victim still awaits vengeance for his untimely death. Defiantly, he issues a bold invitation that the commander join him for supper (3.11). Although Don Juan does not yet realize it, he has taken the first step into the metaphysical world. He becomes aware of this later that night when he hears a knock at his door ("mal da testimonio") and the statue enters (3.13). As it advances to the center of the stage, Don Juan holds a candle in one hand, as if to seek the light of understanding, and a sword in the other, as he attempts to ward off spiritual attack. In this scene, the visual devices ably reflect the spiritual turmoil that Don Juan is experiencing.

Being a good host, Don Juan tries to entertain his supernatural guest as if the social occasion were completely normal. He supplies food and calls for his musicians to provide music. Their offering is a song that affirms the libertine's creed.

> *Si de mi amor aguardáis,*
> *señora, de aquesta suerte*
> *el galardón en la muerte,*
> *¡Qué largo me lo fiáis!*   (3.13)

All the while, the timorous Catalinón alludes to Gonzalo's spiritual state ("es gente de otro país") as he urges his master to realize that the man of the spirit (Gonzalo) is stronger than the man of the flesh. His message is contained in metaphors: "Hombre es de mucho valor, / él es piedra, tú eres carne" (3.13).

In the next scene, Don Juan quizzes his guest to ascertain his true nature—whether he is in a condemned or blessed state. In the following lines, the fearful libertine paraphrases his doubts.

> *¿qué quieres,*
> *sombra o fantasma o visión?*
> *si andas en pena o si aguardas*
> *alguna satisfacción.*
> . . . .
> *¿Estás gozando de Dios?*
> *¿Dite la muerte en pecado?*
> *Habla, que suspenso estoy.*   (3.14)

The commander, who until now has communicated only by nodding his head, reaches out to take Don Juan's hand and urge him to dine in the cemetery the next night. As soon as the invitation is accepted, the statue leaves without the benefit of light, explaining, "en gracia estoy." This action is another affirmation of his supernatural powers.

Alone, Don Juan comtemplates the significance of the visit, admitting that it filled him with fear, especially when he touched Gonzalo's hand: "un infierno parecía" (3.15). The fright soon passes and Don Juan rationalizes that only the living are cause for fear. With a clever pun, he explains his position, proving once again that his heart is still hardened against God.

> *el temor y temer muertos*
> *es más villano temor,*
> *que si un cuerpo noble vivo*
> *con potencias y razón*
> *y con alma, no se teme,*
> *¿quién cuerpos muertos temió?*   (3.15)

The second cemetery scene presents both the spiritual and physical future (3.20). When Don Juan arrives at the tomb, servants clad in mourning bring chairs. The significance of their costumes could be interpreted as mourning either for the commander's unavenged death or for Don Juan's soul. The supper that is served is symbolic of Hell and Satan, for they bring forth scorpions, vipers, asps, stew of nails, and a wine of gall and vinegar. In addition, a chorus sings of the danger of repenting too late.

> *Adviertan los que de Dios*
> *juzgan los castigos grandes,*
> *que no hay plazo que no llegue*
> *ni dueda que no se pague.*
> ....
> *Mientras en el mundo viva,*
> *no es justo que diga nadie:*
> *¡Qué largo me lo fiáis,*
> *siendo tan breve el cobrarse!*   (3.20)

In structure, this allegorical scene is a replica of the one at Don Juan's home, but the implications are reversed. Don Juan accented the pleasures of the moment, while the statue constantly refers to eternal values; however, both allegories present spiritual concepts in concrete terms.

Again Gonzalo reaches for Don Juan's hand, saying, "no temas la mano darme." In spite of this veiled warning, the arrogant young man reaches out his hand (the final rejection of God). Immediately he is overcome by the intensity of the flames that are emitted from Gonzalo's hand; whereupon, the commander explains the symbolism of the fire in a religious image that alludes to God's vengeance.

> *Este es poco*
> *para el fuego que buscaste.*
> *Las maravillas de Dios*
> *son, Don Juan, investigables,*

y así quiere que tus culpas
a manos de un muerto pagues.   (3.20)

Too late, Don Juan realizes the necessity of repentance; therefore, when he begs for confession and absolution, it is denied: "Ya acuerdas tarde." Writhing in pain, Juan moans, "¡Qué me quemo! ¡Qué me abraso! / ¡Muerto soy!" As the libertine who overextended God's grace dies, Gonzalo repeats the moralizing theme: "Esta es justicia de Dios: / quien tal hace, que tal pague" (3.20). The sepulcher holding the bodies of both Don Juan and the commander sinks beneath the stage in a visual confirmation of Don Juan's damnation.

CONCLUSION

This study has concentrated on the religious imagery contained in a large number of Tirso de Molina's plays in an effort to establish the religious intent of the playwright. Imagery is a term used to refer to the body of images contained within literary works. Usually conceived as a verbal art, imagery may include not only verbal images, often referred to as tropes, but also techniques and nonverbal presentations that are used to create visual, mental, or emotional images. A nonverbal approach is used to great advantage in theatrical works.

The images receiving attention in this study are considered under three main classifications: verbal, allegorical, and scenic images. As the category implies, verbal images are those images spoken by the characters in the plays. They may be freestanding or closely tied to nonverbal images within the works. Verbal images, as all images, attempt to capture the essence of an object or sensory experience and express it in terms of an already known experience or situation. They may be literal or figurative in concept.

An allegory can be viewed as an extended metaphor. Tirso certainly saw it as such, for in the concluding lines of his allegory *El Colmenero divino* he announces, "Y la metáfora acabe / de Dios Colmenero" (1.159b). In an allegory, the characters, actions, and events all have meanings independent of the surface story. This deeper level of meaning is the soul of the work. Because allegories present abstractions in the form of concrete images, they are often used for teaching or expounding upon moral or religious principles. Parables, fables, exemplum, and apologues are types of allegories. Tirso de Molina's *autos sacramentales* are classic examples of this dual-level form.

In the theater, the playwright is free to use a number of scenic effects and devices to create images or support other images. These effects include lighting, costuming, music, staging, props, and special effects, such as a flaming sword, the levitation of a body, or the fiery pit of Hell. Image-making scenic techniques and devices, used alone, can produce striking images; used in conjunction with verbal images, they extend and highlight or reinforce the spoken images.

The *autos sacramentales*, allegorical representations of the sacrament of the Eucharist, constitute a significant part of Tirso's theater. Tirso created and supported the allegory through a variety of images: verbal, visual, and aural. All of the characters are symbols, and their symbolism is initially revealed to the audience by means of costuming and well-placed verbal images. In production, additional images, both verbal and scenic, reinforce the religious interpretation of the characters. Within the *autos sacramentales* Tirso presents lavish allegorical scenes, thus creating allegories within the main allegory. These scenes rely heavily on scenic devices for the presentation of religious images. Costuming, staging, props, and music merge to present moving visual and mental images of the Holy Sacrament. In many instances scenic devices and/or costuming could succinctly create the image, but Tirso re-embroiders his scenes with abundant traditional, religious images—some quite extended in form, while others are noteworthy for their brevity.

Tirso produced his first *auto sacramental* in 1613. In subsequent years he wrote four more, the last one bearing the date 1638. Tirso's affinity for this type of allegorical, religious theater continued throughout his dramatic career as the above dates indicate. It is also evident upon examining his other plays that he often incorporated into them image-making techniques and stylistics of the *autos*. For example, tradition deemed that the characters in the *autos sacramentales* serve as symbols, a tradition that Tirso faithfully followed in his own *autos sacramentales*. Tirso also introduced this technique in many of his other plays, creating characters that served as symbols: of religious leaders, humanity, the devil, the Holy Spirit, piety, redemption, and the like. After the characters' symbolism is initially established, usually verbally, their very presence onstage silently continues the image and sustains the desired tone of the play. Allegorical scenes, costuming, and other scenic devices reminiscent of the *autos sacramentales* regularly appear throughout the years in Tirso's fully developed theater.

The hagiographic and biblical plays studied in the second and third chapters represent another facet of Tirso's dramatic personality as he uses imagery to create and sustain a religious aura in his theater. These plays, based on the lives of saints or incidents from the Bible, are written on a more sophisticated level stylistically than the *autos* and, thus, seem to be directed toward a more educated audience. While the *autos* rely heavily on visual symbolism and allegory, these plays are infused with elaborate verbal imagery and are less concerned with the visual. The visual has not been abandoned, only relegated to a position behind that of verbal imagery in most cases. Similes, metaphors, and other allusions to religious subjects appear throughout these plays and exhibit Tirso's ability to create complex images steeped in the literary style of the day. He regularly and skillfully makes use of oxymorons, alliteration, polipote, puns, catachresis, parallel phrasing, and so forth. He creates many of these images along antithetical lines. Particularly in the hagiographic (as well as in the philosophic) plays, images of antithetical nature abound as Tirso establishes the wide chasm that separates Man from God, Heaven from earth. On occasion this distance is symbolized by a secondary plot that is diametrically opposed to the main one. Other times, as in *La Santa Juana: Part III*, the antithesis is visually presented to prepare the audience for forthcoming events. But even as the more complex religious images become apparent, simpler images coexist as if to restate the concepts on a more basic level.

Several of the hagiographic plays call for complex or lavish staging. Usually in the third act, as the play moves toward the climax and rapid denouement, there is an increasing use of allegorical scenes, scenic devices, music, and symbolic costuming to accent the religious character of the story and emotionally prepare the audience for the moralizing conclusion. In these scenes, the pageantry of the *autos* is recalled visually, verbally, and aurally as the images highlight the religiosity of the play. This total dramatic approach to imagery is at its zenith in the final act of *La Santa Juana: Part II*.

Viewing the biblical plays, it is evident that the more inherently religious the story, the fewer images occur. However, when the theme is basically profane, as in *La mujer que manda en casa*, images of religious nature are profuse and varied. Jezebel's idolatry is constantly contrasted in verbal images with the religious fervor of the Fathers of the Church, and allegorical scenes are again prominent in an effort to keep the spiritual element uppermost in the mind of the audience. Staging, props, music, and costuming join to give added reinforcement. In contrast, Tirso's other biblical plays are less elaborate in imagery. An occasional allegorical scene may appear, but the majority of imagery is contained in brief verbal statements, many of which are simple paraphrases of God or the biblical characters featured in the drama. By comparison, the biblical plays are less complex in structure and imagery than are the hagiographic plays. Notwithstanding, there are sufficient verbal images and brief allegorical scenes of religious implication to support the claim that Tirso de Molina used religious imagery in his biblical plays for means of religious edification.

In subject matter the historic-religious plays bear a strong resemblance to the hagiographic plays, although they are not limited to recounting the lives of saints as are the latter. In the face of this similarity, it is logical to anticipate comparable dramatic techniques in the structuring of the imagery. Such is the case. As in the hagiographic plays, the subject matter rarely veers far from the religious, and when it does Tirso is adept at inserting appropriate images so that the spiritual is not forgotten. When verbal images would intrude on a profane scene, he seeks alternative images, many times creating them with costuming, staging, or music. Elsewhere, when the scenes are more spiritually oriented, elaborate verbal analogies and antithetical images are quite prominent. Complete allegorical scenes similar to those found in some of the hagiographic plays also appear on occasion. This is vividly exemplified in the concluding scenes of *Doña Beatriz de Silva* and *Las quinas de Portugal*, where elaborate sets create striking religious images while costuming and music underline the theological message. Combined with the image-laden dialogue, these scenes give an impression of rich pageantry.

The philosophic-religious plays considered in the last chapter of this study represent some of Tirso's finest poetry as well as some of his most refined religious imagery. *El condenado por desconfiado*, allegorical in tone from the outset, is burgeoning with religious images of the highest caliber, ranging from the simplest metaphor to extended, complex, allegorical scenes that are replete with verbal, visual, and musical reinforcement. Costuming, scenic devices, and music are brought into play in a variety of ways: to anticipate verbal images, to underline verbal images, and to create images of a visual, nonverbal character. This multilevel approach to imagery is seen again quite clearly in the final scenes of *El burlador de Sevilla*. The approach is not atypical, as this study has repeatedly noted. Tirso used the same techniques, perhaps with less sustained artistic success, in many of his other plays.

The plays viewed in this study typify Tirso de Molina's theater and are representative of his entire play-writing years. Works under consideration are taken from the early, middle, and later years of his dramatic career, all of which support the claim that religious intent was not sporadic, but rather a general trend within the theater of the priest-playwright. Tirso's religious intent is communicated in large part by means of a variety of images designed to instill theological truths and foster religious devotion. The regularity and frequency with which these religious images appear in Tirso de Molina's plays indicate that his interest was to use the theater not only as a medium of artistic expression but as a vehicle to communicate religious precepts and explore Christian philosophical concepts.

SESQUICENTENNIAL SERIES

In its 150 years, Mercer University has pursued the objectives of excellent teaching and superior scholarship by fostering research in a community dedicated to fresh, original thought. As the University celebrates 150 years of academic leadership, one recognition of this milestone is the publication of the Mercer Sesquicentennial Monograph Series by Mercer University Press.

These three volumes, authored by Mercer faculty members, demonstrate the depth and breadth of the school's dedication to its objectives. Focusing on "excellence in scholarship," the Sesquicentennial Series is another example of the University's commitment to research, scholarship, and publication.

In *Religious Imagery in the Theater of Tirso de Molina* Ann Nickerson Hughes studies the drama of Gabriel Téllez, a Mercederian friar who wrote under the name Tirso de Molina. Many of Tirso's fellow clergymen objected to his plays because of they supposed them to be profane. In 1625, these objections resulted in an order from the Council of Castile prohibiting Tirso from writing plays.

Professor Hughes analyzes Tirso's imagery and argues that the strongest influences on his plays were religious, not secular. She discusses verbal, allegorical, and scenic imagery in five types of plays by Tirso: the *auto sacramentales*, the hagiographic, the biblical, the historic-religious, and the philosophic-religious. As Professor Hughes examines these works, Tirso's consistent use of religious imagery becomes evident. This interest in using the theater to express his religious beliefs was not limited to one period of his career. Consequently, his drama can be seen as representative of the baroque age in which he lived—an age that returned to the religion of the Middle Ages with its strong emphasis on the mystical and spiritual. Tirso was not a rebel working against these values; he was a supporter of these values who used his talent in the theater to persuade sinners to come to salvation and avoid everlasting damnation.

Ann Nickerson Hughes is associate professor of foreign languages at Mercer University in Macon. A graduate of Mercer University, Professor Hughes earned the Ph.D. degree in Spanish literature at the University of Georgia. This is her first book for Mercer University Press.

MUP *Religious Imagery in the Theater of Tirso de Molina*
Binding designed by Alesa Jones and Margaret Jordan Brown
Interior typography design by Margaret Jordan Brown
Composition by MUP Composition Department
Production specifications:
    text paper—60 pound Warren's Olde Style
    endpapers—Multicolor Antique Thistle
    cover—(on .088 boards) Spine Joanna Eton #10500 (gray); Front and Back
    Joanna Eton #19990 (black)
Printing (offset lithography) by Omnipress of Macon, Inc., Macon, Georgia
Binding by John H. Dekker and Sons, Inc., Grand Rapids, Michigan